The Essential Guide to San Diego Real Estate

Insights from San Diego County's Top Agents

Deb Espinoza
Charles Moore
Farryl Moore
Paul Jacinto
Ron Greenwald
Patti Gerke
Scott Voak
David Rudd
Emily Hervieux
Maggie Clemens

Copyright © 2017 NMG Publishing

All rights reserved. No portion of this book may be reproduced mechanically, electronically or by any other means without the expressed written permission of the publisher, except as provided by the United States of America copyright law.

Published by NMG Publishing, Charlotte, North Carolina. The authors and publisher have strived to be as accurate and complete as possible in the creation of this book.

This book is not intended for use as a source of legal, accounting, or financial advice. The information in this book is intended to provide basic information on the topics covered and is not intended to be comprehensive by any means. All readers are advised to seek legal and financial advice from competent professionals, including real estate agents or brokers, when making decisions related to any real estate purchase, sale, or investment, or any other topics covered in this book. The authors and publisher are not responsible or liable for any damages or negative consequences to any person reading or following the information in this book.

The opinions expressed in this book are not those of the publisher. Each co-author contributed to this book in their own personal capacity and the views they have expressed in this book are their own individual views, not the views of the publisher, nor of the other co-authors.

A REALTOR® is a real estate professional who is a member of the National Association of REALTORS® and subscribes to the association's Code of Ethics. The word REALTOR® is not used to describe a person working in the real estate field who is not a member of the National Association of REALTORS®. Although it is acknowledged that the word REALTOR® is trademarked in full capital letters, for the sake of readability, the publisher has spelled it as "Realtor" in this book.

While all attempts have been made to verify information provided in this publication, the authors and publisher assume no responsibility for errors, omissions, or contrary interpretation of the subject matter herein. Any perceived slights of specific persons or organizations are unintentional.

Any trademarks mentioned in this book are listed for reference purposes only and are the property of the respective trademark owners.

Table of Contents

Introduction 1

Deb Espinoza: 3
Buying and Selling Homes in Ramona and
Northeast San Diego County

Charles & Farryl Moore: 25
Buying and Selling Homes in Carmel Valley

Paul Jacinto: 41
Buying and Selling Homes in Coastal North
San Diego County

Ron Greenwald & Patti Gerke: 63
Real Estate Transactions for Seniors

Scott Voak: 83
Buying and Selling Homes in North San Diego County

David Rudd & Emily Hervieux: 101
Maximizing the Profit When Selling Your Home

Maggie Clemens: 125
Buying and Selling Homes in La Mesa and
East San Diego County

Introduction

San Diego County is one of the most desirable areas in the entire United States, or the world for that matter, to live, work and play. The majority of the population lives within about fifteen miles of the coast where there is a year-round mild climate. Almost every active outdoor lifestyle can be enjoyed in the county and winter ski resorts are a two to three hour drive away.

With a population of over 1.4 million, San Diego is the eight largest city in the United States. The metro area has approximately 3 million residents. The economy is well diversified with defense contractors and a major U.S Navy presence, as well as high tech and biotechnology companies with major operations in the area.

According to the Greater San Diego Association of REALTORS® there are over 13,000 real estate agent or broker members in the area. The publisher has selected 10 of the top agents and brokers to contribute to this book. Each of the contributors has a high volume of completed transactions, is highly rated by their clients, and is an advocate for their clients' success. Each contributor has provided their insights for real estate buyers and/or sellers in the area. We hope that this book will become a useful reference for consumers interested in buying or selling homes and other residential properties in the greater San Diego area.

NMG Publishing

Buying and Selling Homes in Ramona and Northeast San Diego County

By Deb Espinoza

Introduction

Deb Espinoza has been an entrepreneur most of her working life. She's owned a travel agency and a plant nursery and has always enjoyed the sales, marketing, and service aspects of business. She founded and is the owner of Stage Presence Homes Realty in Ramona, California in the northeastern part of San Diego County. She has been in real estate since 2002. Deb and her team at Stage Presence Homes specialize in helping buyers and sellers in the Ramona and the North and East parts of San Diego County, although they do help clients throughout San Diego County. She likes working with first time homebuyers, educating them on all aspects of home buying for the first time and seeing their excitement when they get the keys to their new home. Deb also enjoys working with move-up sellers because she has developed techniques to make a very complex series of transactions into a mostly stress-free process. The agency also helps investors, generally with single-family residences or smaller multi-family properties. Ramona has become known for its wineries and the agency also helps in the buying and selling of winery property as well as other business properties in the area.

In this chapter Deb Espinoza provides her insights for residential property buyers and sellers in the Ramona and Northeast San Diego area.

Selling Your Ramona or Northeast San Diego County Property

When a homeowner is considering moving in the near future, whether moving up, down, or relocating, it's best to start talking with an agent as soon as you think that you are going to be moving. An experienced agent will be able to point out the little things that that can be done to the property to get it ready for sale and to maximize the sales price and help the house to sell quicker. There are a number of things like painting and landscaping improvements that don't necessarily have to cost a lot, but can help achieve top dollar and attract buyers' offers much faster. A common mistake I see is homeowners deciding to spend a lot of time and money on a number of improvements before talking with an agent about selling the home. What often happens is they make changes or improvements that are not going to get a return on the investment. This can be avoided by working with an experienced agent right upfront, even 6 to 12 months before the time to put the property on the market.

Thinking ahead, after an offer is accepted, the buyer will be having inspections conducted on the property. The inspections will cover the structure as well as electrical, plumbing, and mechanical systems. A termite inspection will also be ordered, as termites and wood rot are common in the area. Rural properties will also likely require well and septic system inspections. Although the seller may have been living in the home for a long time, it is easy to overlook some issues. I suggest that sellers have their own inspections performed prior to listing the property to uncover any hidden problems that will most likely be found by the buyer's inspections. Termite damage is difficult to see and can be expensive to remediate. It's better to know the full situation upfront instead waiting until the buyer's inspection. This allows the seller to fix things before the listing and allows us to get estimates on items that may be an issue and price accordingly. Some buyers and buyers' agents look at the inspection period as a time to re-negotiate the price. In a lot of these cases this will be a deal killer about 15-20 days into escrow, when the buyer is demanding repairs or a reduction in price, and now the seller is in a really tough spot, especially if they have a property on the other side that they are moving to and now everything is in danger of unraveling. Having inspections done up front and presenting to the buyer at time of offer shows the buyer that the seller knows the full condition of the home and that it is priced accordingly.

We can usually get many needed repairs completed in advance cost effectively, using a handyman. Knowing in advance the likely inspection findings and fixing before listing puts the seller in the best negotiation position. If the pre-inspection finds major issues with major systems such that the HVAC system or the roof are on their last legs, we can take that into consideration in the pricing by putting a range on the price. As an example, if the roof is close to needing replacement, we can set one price if it is taken as is, or if the buyer wants it replaced, then the seller will replace it before the close of escrow, but the buyer will pay full price.

Establishing a realistic market price for a property mostly depends on an analysis of the qualities of location, amenities, condition, and how the property compares with other properties in the neighborhood. Each seller is different and another factor is the seller's motivation surrounding the sale. If there is an urgent need for a sale, say within 30 days, the realistic price is most likely going to be lower that if more time is available to wait for the right buyer. Sellers should expect their agent to provide a comprehensive review of recent comparable sales in the immediate area to come up with an estimated market value.

Upgrades can have an affect on pricing; however, when comparing very similar houses in a neighborhood, the difference in upgraded features is not likely to generate much of a price premium. It's more likely that the better features will help the house sell quicker than the similar house. Although property values are generally appreciating over time, the things installed within the house depreciate over time. There may have been a $100,000 kitchen and bath upgrade 10 years ago, but now the appliances are old and design preferences change over time, so it's difficult to get much current value out of an older remodel project.

Sellers typically ask me, "How long will it take to sell my house?" The time required to sell depends on the market, how well the property is priced, as well as the general economic conditions. As this is being written the average time on market is around 35 to 40 days. In the Ramona and Northeast San Diego County area, what I call "starter houses" range up to about $450,000 at this time. If they are priced right and are in good condition those homes are generally going to move very quickly because there are a lot of buyers in that price range. As we move up to another range up to say $750,000, there are fewer buyers that are qualified, so properties will take a bit longer to sell. In this area, as we move to properties above $750,000, that would generally be considered luxury properties, an even longer time frame will be required for a sale. Unique features of the property or a less desirable floor plan can also cause a house to stay on the market for a longer time.

After the property is listed, buyers will start showing interest in viewing the house. I always advise my sellers to leave the house when there's a showing. Let the buyers enjoy your house. From my experience if the seller is in the house, the buyers are uncomfortable and may feel like they can't really look at the entire house. They seem to go through it a lot quicker, because they just feel some tension with the seller being there. On a second or later visit the seller may want to hang around outside the house, because if the buyers have some questions, you will be there to answer them. After an offer is accepted, the buyer will be requesting inspections. I also recommend that sellers not be present for the home inspections, because it easy to say or promise something that in hindsight you wouldn't do. A lot of inspectors will call out things that aren't really big issues and you might go ahead and start fixing things that aren't really necessary. It's just best to let your agent do that work for you and negotiate and take care of those little details, so you're not getting drawn into the things that could hurt you from a negotiating standpoint.

Some sellers want to know if an open house will be used to attract buyers as a thought that it is a good way to get more exposure of the property. It's actually pretty rare to sell a house to someone that visits an open house. Agents generally hold open houses to get exposure for the agent. Most people that come to the open houses are nosey neighbors or neighbors that are looking to possibly sell their property pretty soon and they want to look at the pricing and the competition.

It's an exciting and maybe a nervous time for a seller when their house goes on the market. When a house first goes on the market, that's generally when the most activity happens. There's a pool of buyers out there that have seen everything on the market. They have their money, they're ready to go, but nothing has been available that matches what they're looking for. I always tell my sellers to look carefully at the first offer because in most cases that first offer that you get is going to be your best offer. I suggest countering any offer that comes in, even if it's low-ball. A seller always wants to get the highest price, so respond to the offers and try to reach a deal that will work.

Listing agreements are negotiable between the seller and the agent; however, most real estate agencies operate with a "standard" commission rate. There are some discount agencies out there that provide for a lower than standard selling-side commission rate. I've run some numbers and it's like you've always heard, "You get what you pay for." Discount agents don't really have any budget to market a house; they only list it in the Multiple Listing Service (MLS), put a sign in your yard, and hope that a buyer will see the listing or the sign and show an interest. In today's world, buyers expect to be able to go online and see a good selection of photos inside and outside the property and the discount agent listings generally have a very limited number of poor quality pictures. Discount agents don't do advertising or anything else to get your home in front of enough buyers or the right buyers. They may not properly represent the seller as they just want to get the property sold at any price and may even advise to take any offer on the table. I ask sellers, "Do you want to pay a little higher commission and get over 99% of your list price, or risk getting the area average of 95-97%?" The net to the seller is higher taking into account an agent who gets 99% of your list price and is a great negotiator compared to going for a discount agent based on commission alone.

Contrast with the marketing that professional real estate agencies like ours does for your property. What's going to catch the eye of the buyer is those homes that are showing up on paid websites like Zillow, Trulia, and Realtor.com with great high definition photography, that's going to show off the home in good color and proper perspective. It's going to include virtual tours and comprehensive descriptions. The other point is to get your house in front of as many people as possible so our marketing may also include paid advertising on Facebook and print marketing. There is also going to be someone to answer the phones and take care of questions.

One of my specialties is working with sellers that want to also purchase another house in the area. A common issue is timing everything so that funds from the sale of the existing home will take care of the down payment on the new home. This is a complicated situation because sellers don't like contingent offers that require the buyer's house to be sold before closing on the purchase. They don't want to take their house off the market for something that might not happen.

We have a solution for our sellers that puts them into the driver's seat. We do this by structuring the offers and counteroffers that makes the seller's home sale contingent upon finding a replacement home that the seller likes in a specific amount of time. In this way the seller is in a great negotiating position to make an offer on a new home as the existing home already is under contract. By putting the protections in, you can abandon the contract on your existing house if a suitable new home is not found. This is a preferred position compared to contracting to purchase a new property first and then stressing to try to sell the existing house, likely below market, just to get it sold.

What Sellers Are Saying

"I have bought and sold many homes throughout my life and have never experienced such a professional, objective and successful selling experience. Deb was very straight forward and honest in providing us guidance on what we needed to do to present our home in the best light. She was also very responsive to any concerns we had along the way. She also took the time to share with us in reviewing other properties in our neighborhood in the same price range. Thereby allowing us to price the house accordingly . . . in the sweet spot. Bottom line, the house sold in one week. We are very pleased. We would absolutely do business with Deb Espinoza again and we highly recommend her to all of our friends."

- Bob & Barb W.

"There are not words to describe how great Deb Espinoza is! I have sold many properties in my lifetime and never have I had such a wonderful experience as with Deb. She has deep knowledge of the entire San Diego County Real Estate Market. The house she helped me sell in Vista was in need of so much repair I could never have sold it on my own. She hooked me up with a Contractor who did the needed repairs on my house, and the result was that 4 different buyers wanted my house immediately! She is completely accessible, returns phone calls right away, and always lets you know exactly what is happening at all times. I would highly recommend her for all your real estate needs!"

- MaryBeth G.

"Our home was listed with another Realtor for one year and not one offer was presented. Within five days of listing with Deb, we were

presented with three offers. Our home is now sold! Deb identified some minor improvements that were necessary and served as a project manager to make sure the improvements were completed in a timely manner. Her attention to every detail was amazing and her communication throughout our listing exceeded my expectations. I have worked with many Realtors in multiple states and I have to say Deb is the best by far! I would recommend her without reservation."

-Mark M.

Buying Your Ramona or Northeast San Diego County Property

One of the first steps a buyer should take before starting to search for a house is to get the financing set up beforehand. One reason for this is that when working with a lender, they will pull your credit report and in many cases, there will be errors in the credit report that will cause a score to be lower than it should be. It can take at least 30 days to get any errors resolved, so being proactive you and your lender can get issues solved right upfront and not cause delays later in the process. Another key point is to be able to know for sure the maximum loan amount you will be able to obtain. The loan officer will also review other aspects of your credit and may have simple suggestions on some things the buyer can do to raise the credit score, thus qualifying for a better rate or a larger loan amount. It's a good time to also start working with an agent because many agents can refer buyers to lenders that have experience and reputation of being able to close on time, and a broad range of available loans, with varying down payment terms.

Another reason is that sellers want to work with buyers that are pre-approved for financing. If you go and make an offer on your dream house and it takes you a few days to obtain approval from the lender, the house may be gone by the time you get the approval. It's always best to get your ducks in a row and have your pre-approval done so that you go out fully prepared. If you find a property you love, an offer can be made, with the seller knowing you are qualified for the financing.

Some people think they will need as much as 20% down payment to purchase a house, but that's not necessarily the case. The amount of money that's going to be needed to close on a property will depend primarily on the type of financing used. This is another reason to start working with a lender and an agent as early as possible in the process. There are a number of options that provide 100% or close to 100% financing, so no down payment or very little down payment is possible. If you're a military veteran or you're in the reserves, you can qualify for VA financing, which is 0% down and no mortgage insurance. If you have really good credit, even with a conventional loan you can put as little as three to five percent down. In Ramona we have what's called a USDA Rural Loan with 100% financing. There are also some programs for community service professions like teachers, firefighters, and police officers where grants are available that provide up to 103% financing so not only is there no down payment required, but also funds to cover other closing costs.

When working with our preferred lenders, buyers will receive a statement of estimated closing costs needed at the time of approval so they will know exactly what will be needed. Sometimes buyers are saving up enough for the down payment on an FHA loan that requires 3-1/2% and that's all they have, not realizing that additional funds are likely needed at closing. In this case we may ask for a little help from the seller in a closing cost credit. We might offer a little bit more on the house so that the seller can give back a little bit at closing to help pay for closing costs.

If you haven't already started working an agent, once you're pre-approved and are ready to look for a house to purchase, it's time to identify an agent to help you with your home search and transaction. With all of the online listings some people think that they shouldn't start working with an agent to represent them until they see a home they are interested in. One issue with this is that you are not likely to find all of the available houses online. There are a lot of hidden listings that are not shown on the MLS for a variety of reasons and experienced agents are likely to have some of these or have relationships with other agents that have access to them. You won't have access to these properties that might meet your exact needs unless working with an active, experienced agent.

A misconception some buyers have is that by working directly with a listing agent, they will be able to get a better deal. Technically, the listing agent is the fiduciary of the seller. If they are an ethical agent, they are not going to give the buyer any kind of information to indicate the seller's negotiating position, so if you work directly with the listing agent, no one is negotiating on your behalf. When a home is listed the seller pays the listing broker a certain percentage of the sales price (commission) and from that commission the listing broker pays the broker that brings a buyer, so in most cases it costs a buyer nothing to have their own representation. Also, if there is any savings realized by the buyer being represented by the seller's agent, the seller will reap that reward, not the buyer, because the agent's first fiduciary duty is to the seller. By working with an agent to represent you, you'll be able to have someone negotiating specifically on your behalf.

The Ramona and surrounding rural area is a unique market and understanding the characteristics of the area is critical for deciding what to offer for a property. There aren't many tract housing developments, so everything is pretty much custom and there can be a big difference in value in two houses situated next to each other. Working with an agent that knows the area well will help you establish an appropriate offer. Some areas are more desirable than others and an experienced local agent that focuses on the specific area will be frequently running comps and will have more detailed knowledge of property values. An agent with better knowledge of the local market will be able to assess the inventory and know how well the property is priced. If it is priced well, you run the risk of multiple offers such that the seller will not even counter your offer if it is too low.

With the Ramona area being an attractive rural alternative to the urbanized areas of San Diego County, I am seeing a lot of interest in more people desiring to move to the area. The rural environment, however, involves some different perspectives on public utilities than people coming from the urban areas are familiar with. Except for right in town, most properties will have a private well and septic system. There are no natural gas lines here so we use propane heating. In making an offer the buyer needs to take into consideration inspections and well water testing for these systems (and an experienced agent will know how to read and interpret the results). On a number of occasions I have listed a house here, and agents not familiar with the area helped their buyers put in offers that did not protect them with respect to contingencies for the rural utility systems. Again, another reason to work with an experienced local agent.

After you come to agreement with a seller on a purchase offer you will have a contingency period to perform inspections and to get the financing finalized.

An inspection involves hiring a neutral third-party to check the house and provide a report on the condition of the home that you're purchasing. They will be checking the roof, foundation, heating and air conditioning systems, all the appliances, water heater, electrical, and plumbing, making sure everything is in good condition and working properly. Additional inspections may also include a termite inspection and well and septic checks, if applicable. As an agent for the buyer, I take care of setting up the inspections. The inspector I work with also gives tips on maintenance for the homeowner and that's something that first time homebuyers find very helpful. If the inspection results show some issues with the property, there can be additional negotiations with the seller to correct items noted or to reduce the property price to reflect the problems noted. There's another thing for a buyer to note about the inspection. A home inspection is not intended for cosmetic issues or for replacing old systems that may be 'past life,' but still working properly. Offers are made based on the current condition of the property at time of the offer, and we make sure all our buyers are provided with a one-year home warranty to cover all systems in the home, so if something does fail it will be repaired or replaced for a small service charge. We recommend our buyers keep these warranties renewed annually to avoid any surprise large cost repairs that may not be budgeted for.

As part of the financing process, the lender will order an appraisal of the property being purchased. The lender is going to be looking at the collateral for the loan and they want to make sure that the appraisal values the property for as much as they are lending on. As part of the process they will be checking the condition of the house to make sure that there's no partially completed construction, the roof is in good condition, there is no evidence of termite damage, or rotted wood that would devalue the property.

On a fairly negotiated property deal, the appraisal usually supports the purchase price, but sometimes that is not the case. If the buyer is using an FHA or VA loan with very low or no down payment and the appraisal doesn't support the price, the buyer's agent is generally going to have to go back to the seller to show the appraisal and request the price to be lowered. Otherwise there will not be a deal. There is more flexibility on conventional funding with a large down payment. In this case the buyer can go to the seller and request a price reduction, but the seller can say they are not going to reduce the price to the level of the appraisal. In this case if the seller holds firm on the price, the buyer can either accept the price that is higher than appraisal if they really love the property, or they can decide to walk away.

What Buyers Are Saying

"Deb and her team were absolutely amazing. Seriously; this is the first time I have actually believed that my agent was on our side from the get go. I hate the buying experience, I hate searching, I hate negotiating... BUT; within the first few hours spending some time with Deb I felt totally comfortable giving her the reins to make the calls on my behalf. Start to Finish, this is the FIRST time buying a home was actually NOT what I had to spend every waking minute trying to manage. You're awesome Deb and everyone in your office was spectacular! Our dream of moving to Ramona..... Check that off the list!"

- Eric G.

"YOU SHOULD CALL DEBBIE ESPINOZA- there is a reason that she has all 5 star ratings! Deb is an AMAZING broker. She made me feel as if I were the only client that she had and I am not the easiest person to work with as I was super anxious

about finding and getting into our new home. There was never a moment that I couldn't reach her, and no question seemed to be insignificant to her. I am clear that I would recommend her again and again for anyone who was buying a home. THANK YOU Deb for your crazy level of support and professionalism."

- Paula R.

"I met Deb early on in my process of buying a home and she helped me for 2 years before I was ready and able to buy. She put me on a list of daily updated that met the requirements I had wanted and all along devoted time and energy to my questions while I learned the process and was finally able to commit to buying. At that time the process rapidly sped up of looking at homes and finally she helped me find just the right one. Even when I thought the deal was a good one she even pushed for things I was not aware of. I don't know what buyers remorse is because I was so well educated by Deb by the end and wound up with more than I could have expected. The process was sometimes scary as a first time buyer but she made it so much fun that I feel like I have a friend as well by the end of this process. Deb gets the highest rating from me across the board! I'm a home owner! Woohoo! Thanks so much Deb. It was fun."

-Tim H.

How to Select the Best Agent

Buying and selling a home is one of the largest financial transactions a family or individual will make in their life. Whether you are a buyer or a seller, it is important to pick an agent to work with that is well equipped to handle the entire process professionally and to provide you with the best possible results. First, I would recommend working with a full time agent that has made a career of helping others with their real estate transactions. I would check the track record and that it shows a good volume of closed transactions. Local knowledge is very important, especially in unique markets like Ramona and the Northeast San Diego County area.

When selling, you want to have an agent with a team that can take care of all of the details, someone that it's their full time commitment to get the property sold. I recommend checking the record of ratio of actual sales price to listing price, as this is generally a good indicator of the negotiation skills. Ask the agent how they will be marketing the house and exposing it to potential buyers. The best methods are generally going to include online paid advertising on real estate sites as well as print ads. As mentioned before, professional photography is important to attract the attention of buyers searching online.

There are a lot of people involved in successfully selling a house, from inspectors, photographers, the title and escrow company, the buyer's agent, lenders, and others. The seller needs to have someone that can handle all of the coordination. Selling a house is a stressful situation and ongoing communication is important to make sure you know what is happening with the process. When a potential buyer calls and wants to see the house, make sure the agent or a team member is going to be available to set the appointment or handle a showing.

My personal philosophy and that of my team is to work as a concierge service for our clients. We like working with clients that want to be taken care of and want us to handle all of the details. We'll set up appointments and be there for the inspections. We'll take care of getting bids for repairs. We go through and explain the paperwork, making sure they have a full grasp on what's going on at every stage of the process. We educate so that they can make the decisions on their own. Our sellers are in charge and it's their house. It's our job to show the comps with all of the backup data and to guide them in determining the right price. We want our clients to be confident that we are working in their best interests, are going to get the best price, and get it sold in within our clients' timeframe. It's not just getting the house on the market, and getting it sold. I'm interested in long-term client relationships and that my clients can trust me with a very important transaction.

Ramona and Northeast San Diego County

Ramona is a beautiful unincorporated area about 45 minutes northeast of downtown San Diego. Ramona is what can best be described as a "bedroom community" of San Diego. It's a town with a rural character and most properties are on acreage without any real "cookie cutter" homes. It's a community with a lot of events that bring families together such as the Country Fair, Rodeo, 4th of July Fireworks, parades, and 4-H. During Ramona Graffiti Cruise Nights, families come out and line Main Street to watch the classic cars cruise up and down until the sun goes down.

Ramona is also becoming well known as San Diego's hot spot for wine tasting as boutique family-run wineries are popping up all over the area. Locals and "down-the-hill" tasters come together over a great glass of wine and great stories the local vintners tell of how they got started and how their particular varieties of wine are made. An atmosphere like this makes Ramona the town where you can go into the grocery store or a local restaurant and say "hi" to several people that you know. Local home prices are quite a bit more affordable than "down-the-hill" and very much worth it for someone willing to add a few minutes to their commute. Many homeowners enjoy the commute as it gives them time to decompress after a day at work as they drive up into their country town.

About Deb Espinoza

Deb Espinoza and her husband Joe have been married for 31 years and have two sons, Zach & Ross, two beautiful daughters-in-law and currently two grandkids that have their hearts - Joey and Eleanor. Both Deb and Joe are native San Diegans, and moved to Ramona in 1988. Deb has lived and sold in many areas of San Diego County and is very familiar with most cities and neighborhoods.

Deb is active in her church and sings on the worship team. She also enjoys gardening, travel, reading, and spending time with family and friends.

Deb currently serves on the Ramona Real Estate Association board as treasurer; she was also vice president of the San Diego Seller Representative Specialist (SRS) board. Deb and Stage Presence Homes Realty support local high school sports, the local 4th of July event, Ramona Food & Clothes Closet, her local church, and Friends of Ramona Unified Schools (FORUS).

Deb feels that continuing education is paramount to providing her clients the best service and to the success of her business. She holds a GRI designation (a year+ long program of real estate classes designed to give a broad knowledge of all aspects of real estate), Seller Representative Specialist (SRS), Accredited Buyer Representative (ABR), Certified Negotiation Expert (CNE), Accredited Staging Representative, Certified in Feng Shui, and is a member of the National Association of Expert Advisors. Deb is a multi-year winner of the Top San Diego Real Estate Agent 5 Star Award for Excellence in customer service as featured in San Diego Magazine, was recognized as a Gold recipient of San Diego real estate's Circle of Excellence Award for production, and has been featured in San Diego's Top Agent Magazine.

For more information about Deb Espinoza and Stage Presence Homes Realty, visit http://www.StagePresenceHomes.com.

Buying and Selling Homes In Carmel Valley

By Charles and Farryl Moore

Introduction

Charles Moore has been an entrepreneur his entire career and Farryl Moore worked for Nordstrom's before entering the real estate industry 14 years ago. Charles recognized the opportunities presented by the real estate field and 12 years ago he decided to join Farryl in real estate. He observed at the time that a professional business approach was mostly missing from the real estate industry at the time, so he and Farryl put together a business plan where they could succeed with a focused approach that would provide outstanding customer service for their clients. They have lived in Carmel Valley since 1988 and they believed that a primary focus on the area they know best, Carmel Valley, ZIP Code 92130, would provide unsurpassed expertise for buyers and sellers.

In this chapter Charles and Farryl provide insights for both homebuyers and sellers in Carmel Valley.

Selling Your Carmel Valley Home

When you know that you're going to be moving it's best to meet with an agent a few months in advance so that you can be getting prepared for marketing your home. A key attraction to Carmel Valley is the quality of the local schools so there's a lot a buying activity centered on the school schedule. February through June is a prime time to list a property because many buyers are looking in the spring and typically want to move in before September when school is starting. We send out a flyer to people in the area in December and let them know that if they plan to market their home in the first six months of the year we should meet with them in December or January. We like to meet to discuss timing and any changes that should be made to merchandise the home so we can get top value. Sometimes sellers have in their mind that a number of changes are needed to maximize the value, and it's not necessarily true, so we also like to go over what shouldn't or isn't important to change, because otherwise money can be wasted.

An important factor in getting the top price for a home is properly pricing it for the market. Every home is different and even the valuation techniques used in a typical Competitive Market Analysis (CMA) may not be as accurate as it can be. The first step is a macro view of the area, in this case for ZIP Code 92130. We like to review all sales in the area in the past 3 months, 6 months, and last year as well as how many homes are currently on the market. We then take it down to the subdivision level and look at the sales on a price per square foot range.

Next we look at other factors that can make a home more or less valuable. The specific school assignment for the property is a key factor as well as location amenities or location liabilities. A great view or a superior yard can add as much as 10% to the value, while having a busy road right behind the home can reduce the value by as much as 10%. Of course, quality of construction as well as level and age of improvements and remodels are also important elements of a home's value. This is a little more scientific than the normal CMA, but it will leave a seller with enough information to know as much as anyone about the estimated market value of the home.

Timing the sale is almost as important as the price in obtaining top dollar for a home in the area. We mentioned earlier about the quality of the schools being a driving force in the Carmel Valley marketplace. Timing the sale to coincide with when buyers with children want to move is a key point. If you come on the market around February or March you'll likely get as much as 8% more than if you were to list in September or October. Of course it also depend upon how much inventory comes on the market between March and June.

Carmel Valley has been a very active market for the past few years and homes that are priced right, in good condition, and listed in the prime selling season sell quickly. A home in the area priced under $1 million will typically sell within 10 to 15 days. Homes between $1 million and $1.25 million are more likely to take as much as 30 days for a sale. If it's above $1.5 million it can be as much as 2 to 3 months. At higher price points we find fewer qualified buyers.

We both come from a retail merchandizing background and we apply successful strategies from the retail industry to merchandize our listings. When a home goes on the market it needs to look attractive and inviting to buyers and convey the impression that it was well maintained and taken care of.

One of the reasons we like to meet with sellers a few months in advance is to be able to help them prepare the home for sale. This doesn't mean that a lot of money needs to be spent on improvements and, in fact, we generally don't recommend making many changes. It's a matter of what they should do as well as what they shouldn't do. Some sellers think they should change carpeting, but you really can't know what the buyer wants. Maybe they want a different color or they prefer hardwood floors or stone, so new carpeting doesn't give them any value. Most of the time making major changes at this time will not return the money spent because the odds are the buyer would want to change it anyway.

What's really important is a very clean and fresh looking home. Touch-up any paint that has scratches or holes and make sure the carpeting is clean. Repainting should only be considered if a wall is damaged beyond what a touch-up can fix or if there is a bright color that might cause a lot of distraction to some buyers. In this case painting a neutral color is recommended because you don't want to limit who might buy your home.

Most families accumulate a lot of furniture and personal items over the years so it is pretty common to find homes cluttered. Buyers want to imagine how their furniture will fit. Remember, less clutter will make the spaces appear larger. We generally walk through the home room-by-room with the seller and make recommendations on ways to enhance the space to show it in the best manner possible. Generally we're going to advise to de-clutter and de-personalize so that there is some space on mantles, shelves, and walls so buyers walking through the home can imagine living there with their own personal items. Presentation is also a key; that is why we spend so much time making sure the home is perfect before taking professional photographs. We want to showcase the home online and in other advertising looking it's best.

When a buyer visits your home, the first thing they are going to see is the front yard and the front exterior. On the outside of the house the windows should be washed and stucco or siding pressure washed. The landscaping should be trimmed back, weeds removed, shrubs manicured and fresh bark chips placed in planters to cover dirt. We also recommend getting some color on the outside with flowering plants. Be mindful of shrubs or planting too close to the house. Trim back any tree branches touching the roof line as this will prevent damaged roof tiles and critters from finding their way into your attic.

Online exposure is critical, as most buyers will be viewing homes online before deciding which homes to visit. We post our listings to over 900 websites. We look at the online viewing of a home to be the first showing and the second showing is when a buyer walks in your door. If the first showing doesn't attract interest, there most likely won't even be a second showing. They're not going to be emotionally connected to the home by looking at it online; that comes from physically walking through the home. Therefore, it is important to make the online viewing as attractive as possible to get their interest. Professional photography is critical to showcasing the home in the best possible manner. Photos should only be taken after the home is staged and ready for sale; otherwise it may detract from getting that second showing.

One thing we realize is that most people who buy in Carmel Valley already know somebody that lives here and they are attracted to the area due to the schools or other amenities. With that in mind we market a lot to the people already in the area because they likely know someone that would like to move here or they may want to stay in the area and want a larger or smaller home. For that reason we distribute our brochure featuring our listings to people already living here. The brochure also has area information. We also distribute it to medium size and larger companies in the area. When they're recruiting people they will use our brochure to give recruits some ideas about the area. We also believe it's important to do print advertising and we advertise our listings in a number of high-end local publications.

In merchandizing the home we believe that it's critical for the listing agent to be present for all showings instead of placing a lockbox on the front door. We require an appointment for all showings. One reason for this is to be able to get to the home before the showing to turn on the lights, open the blinds, and do anything else that will make the home look it's best.

The other reason is to be able to meet the buyer and buyer's agent to walk them through the home. As we walk them through the home we are able to hear any objections they have and are able to address them before the buyers get back to their car. As an example, if they bring up the fact that a similar property down the street sold for $100,000 lower we are able to address the difference which might be a better view at our listing or maybe the other property was adjacent to a busy street in the back. By focusing our efforts on Carmel Valley we are able to visit almost every home that comes on the market, so we are able to accurately describe the differences. We actually help the buyer's agent sell the home.

What Sellers Are Saying

"We interviewed the top 5 agents in Carmel Valley in anticipation of listing our home for sale. Charles and Farryl immediately impressed us with their in depth knowledge of the neighborhood, in general, and our home in particular. Charles even brought with him the sales flyer from when we purchased our home ten years earlier. Where as other agents gave us over-the-top ideas for staging and preparing our home for sale, the Moores gave us targeted advice which saved us thousands of dollars. Farryl spent several days staging our home herself. Ultimately, they brought us a full-priced offer on the day we listed. We closed escrow less than 45 days later. Throughout the process both Charles and Farryl were extremely professional and responsive. Things simply could not have gone any smoother."

- Nadia K.

Buying Your Carmel Valley Home

The Internet has changed everything when it comes to searching for a new home; searches online now are about 80% of the search process. Buyers can find almost any home that has been listed for sale along with a description and generally a collection of photos on a large number of websites. With all of this information online, many buyers wonder if they should just go ahead and contact the listing agent to show a home that looks good online, and if they like it, to make an offer directly through the listing agent. Certainly that is one approach, but an important point to consider is that the listing agent has a fiduciary responsibility to the seller, so it's difficult to be able to look out for the best interests for both the buyer and seller.

Our recommendation is to work with a qualified buyer's agent to represent you. The best time to select and start working with a buyer's agent is when you have a pretty good idea of the area where you want to buy. Some agents will indicate that they work anywhere within San Diego County (or even beyond); however, we believe you will be best represented by an agent that specializes and has detailed knowledge in a narrower area. Probably the biggest asset of having your own buyer's agent is to protect you and make sure you are making the best purchase for your needs and that you will not be hurt in the long run. It doesn't cost the buyer anything to be represented, as generally half of the sales commission that is being paid by the seller is to pay for the agent on the buyer's side of the transaction.

The buyer's agent is there to provide relevant information about the area, cost factors and differences that may not be apparent, to make sure that the buyer does not overpay, and to protect the buyer during the negotiation and transaction process. Understanding restrictions and fees of a Home Owners Association (HOA) is important from both a cost standpoint as well as flexibility in the manner in which a home is used. There may be restrictions on improvements, so if there is an intention to expand or change the home, one needs to understand the limitations. In California, we have special tax districts for schools known as Mello-Roos. Taxes differ by school district and the tax can be a few thousand dollars per year, on top of property taxes. Detail local knowledge is a real asset when it comes to knowing these differences on a neighborhood-by-neighborhood basis.

It takes a lot of skill and local knowledge to be able to advise on the appropriate price for a home. Some websites provide an estimated value for each home in a neighborhood, but these values are based on algorithms that don't consider many important factors such as condition, improvement level, view, and noise level. Two fairly identical homes across the street from each other may have fairly similar values indicated on the website, but one home may be priced and valued at as much as $200,000 higher than the other. Buying a home is an emotional process and our job as a buyer's agent is to advise on a fair price so you don't end up paying too much. In a time when multiple offers are common you don't want to get too excited that you overpay. We use pretty much the same type of analysis as we would with a seller to determine a fair value, so the buyer will be educated before making an offer they regret later. Of course it's up to the buyer as to what to offer, as agents don't set the price. The price is really what a seller and a buyer agree upon.

Typically the full closing process takes 45 to 60 days. After there is an agreement, the buyer has some time to conduct due diligence and remove contingencies. The typical contract in California allows for 17 days for removal of contingencies other than loan for which 21 days are usually provided. During this time the buyer will have inspections conducted to understand the condition of the structure as well as the mechanical and electrical systems. If major issues are noted in the inspections, the buyer has the ability to get out of the contract; however, most of the time the buyer and seller have some additional negotiations through their agents to reach agreement on making needed repairs before settlement.

Many of the buyers in Carmel Valley are moving from within the San Diego area, so a frequent issue is the sequencing of selling the existing home and buying the new home. With the market being tight, it is very rare that a seller will accept any offer that is contingent on selling an existing home. This can create a dilemma for someone that wants to move. If funds or financing is available to be able to pay for two homes simultaneously, one option is to buy the new home and sell the existing home after finding the new home. Although not very common, we are starting to see some bridge loans, which allow for carrying two properties for a short period of time; however, lenders will be looking for very strong financial capability.

The most practical approach is to get the existing home listed and into escrow and then start looking for a new home. You can require in the sales agreement to rent back your home for a short period of time to allow for finding and closing on a new home. Another alternative is to find another place to rent for a short period of time until a new home is purchased.

What Buyers Are Saying

"Chuck and Farryl helped me find a great property. They also suggested I buy a rental property in a specific zip code. I said no as I wanted to move slower. I wish I had listened to them! The properties in the zip code they suggested had the highest increase in all of San Diego! So listen to their advice! They are also very patient and never make you feel pressured. I have referred other friends to them and everyone is very happy with Chuck and Farryl's attention to detail and negotiating expertise.

Once you know them, they are always there for you. Just this week they spent a lot of their time helping with an elderly relative's real estate transaction and gave detailed written advice, even though this transaction does not involve them. Because they are such skilled negotiators the other side was not happy at the close of escrow with the great deal Chuck and Farryl had achieved for us, but Chuck and Farryl were very kind and managed to smooth things over."

- RK S.

Selecting an Agent

Whether buying or selling, we believe that one of the most important aspects when selecting an agent is the local knowledge along with experience. San Diego County is pretty large and it's difficult to have any detail neighborhood understanding unless an agent is focused on a given area. Years of experience as well the number of successfully closed transactions are also important factors to consider when selecting an agent. In our case we have lived in Carmel Valley since 1988 and focus our work in this area.

When selling, check the level of marketing that's going to be done to effectively present the home to greatest number of qualified buyers. Professional photography using the right lighting effects will show the home at it's best. Is the agent offering staging services? Will there be online and print advertising? How are showings going to be handled? Will there just be a lockbox on the door so any agents can show the home or will your agent be present for all showings? These are some of the things to consider when selecting an agent.

Carmel Valley

Carmel Valley, a neighborhood within the City of San Diego, is ideally located near the coast, just minutes north of downtown. The westernmost part of Carmel Valley is just about a mile from the beach and Torrey Pines State Reserve. The coastal influence keeps the climate moderate and especially as compared to further inland parts of San Diego County.

Families living in Carmel Valley take advantage of very highly rated public schools that are well known for outstanding academics. The Del Mar and Solano Beach elementary school districts serve most of Carmel Valley, while the San Dieguito Union High School District serves middle and high school levels.

The combination of a near-coastal environment, ideal weather and top-notch schools makes Carmel Valley one of the most prized areas to live in in all of Southern California.

About Charles and Farryl Moore

Charles and Farryl Moore are full-time real estate professionals who specialize in Carmel Valley properties. They assist buyers and sellers with all types of homes from condos to luxury estates. They both have strong retail experience and they bring exceptional customer service to every transaction.

Farryl's retail background included 10 years with Nordstrom. She has been in the real estate industry for over 14 years. Farryl is a trained property stager and has the expertise to assist sellers in preparing their homes for the market.

Charles also comes from a retail background. He owned and operated The Athlete's Foot stores, which later merged with Second Sole, and he helped to build a chain of 40 corporate and 40 franchise locations. He then partnered to open a chain of 19 Computerized Cobbler stores. Charles followed Farryl into real estate about 12 years ago.

Charles and Farryl have lived and raised their family in Carmel Valley since 1988. Their three sons attended local schools before attending and graduating from the University of California system. They know the Carmel Valley in detail and have visited most of the homes that have come on the market over the past several years.

Charles and Farryl have won the Coldwell Banker International President's Premier Award, indicating that they are in the Top 1% Internationally. They also hold a number of real estate industry certifications including:
- Certified Residential Specialist
- Previews Specialist
- Accredited Staging Professional
- Certified Negotiation Expert
- Senior Real Estate Specialist
- Accredited Buyer's Representative
- Short Sale and Foreclosure Resource Certification.

For more information about Charles and Farryl Moore, visit www.CarmelValleyHomes.com.

Buying and Selling Homes in Coastal North San Diego County

By Paul Jacinto

"Relationships drive our core business. It is through establishing and strengthening relationships with clients and associates that I am able to exceed client expectations." – Paul Jacinto

Introduction

Paul Jacinto got his start in real estate after college working with a development company in San Diego County. Soon, he became responsible for all property acquisitions as well as asset sales. When the market cooled in 2006 and 2007 the development company owners decided to retrench and wait for a market rebound. Paul turned the market slow-down into an opportunity to launch his own brokerage company with a mission to help individual buyers and sellers achieve their home ownership goals.

The market continued to spiral down for a few years as Paul was growing his real estate business. It was a scramble to start a new business in a down market. At the same time agents were leaving the industry in huge numbers he hustled to meet and gain as many clients as he could, which put him in a great position as the market started to come back in 2012. Paul had built a referral-based business founded on relationships—making and strengthening relationships by providing clients personalized service and exceeding expectations.

In addition to helping his clients with single-family homes, Paul has become an expert in small residential development properties, including buying and selling raw land, as well as property management for condos, small multi-family residential, and small commercial properties. He has also developed more than 12 residences of his own that he now manages.

Paul works with buyers and sellers around San Diego, Orange, and Riverside Counties, with his primary market in the North San Diego County coastal area from Oceanside and Carlsbad to Del Mar. In this chapter, he provides insights for buyers and sellers in the North San Diego County coastal area.

Selling Your Coastal North County Home

An agent's job is to help a client receive "top-dollar" for his or her home. Although it is common for some sellers to wait to contact an agent until they are ready to sell their home, working with an agent in the planning stages will help the seller prepare in advance for such an important decision.

An experienced agent lends expertise by advising clients on three critical factors that will help a client successfully sell his or her home: timing, value, and marketability. By working with an agent before you are ready to list your home, the client can learn when is the best time to sell, what is the value of the property, and how to make the home more marketable.

<u>Timing</u>

You may be asking yourself, "Why is timing so important when selling a home? A home is worth what it is worth; so why does selling a home during July or August make a difference when compared to selling a home in November or December?" The answer is simple economics: supply and demand, and an answer that is driven mostly by demand.

There is very little demand by buyers to make a purchase in November or December; therefore a seller will not receive "top-dollar" for his or her home if there is no demand. On the other-hand, buyers are anxious to make a purchase during the months of July or August, for example, and therefore higher demand creates excitement, which leads to an opportunity for a higher asking price.

Most home sales activity in the San Diego area occurs from January through the end of summer, and is the best time to put a home on the market. During the autumn months through the holiday months, neither buyers nor sellers are motivated to make a move, activity tends to be low, and inventory, as well, tends to be low.

Let a real estate professional advise you on the right time to list your home.

Value

A home's value is determined by location, square footage, lot size, condition, surrounding areas, view, age, interior and exterior upgrades, style, and the current market situation. Identifying an accurate property valuation is an art form, and an experienced agent will be able to use all the different colors (or factors) in all their varied shades to help sellers gain an accurate understanding of what their house is worth. An experienced agent will perform a comparative market analysis, during which the home is compared to a number of recently sold properties that are most similar to the subject property.

When establishing a sale price, at least six recent comparable past property sales, also known as comparables, or "comps," that have sold within the last six months should be included in a market analysis. The analysis should not just be based on past sales, but should also include as a factor current properties for sale that are either pending, or that are actively listed. The analogy of an "art form" continues as an agent must take into account the varying spectrum of colors that determine a sale price, and must help clients understand the reasons that seemingly similar properties are sold at varying prices.

For example, a house with the same floor plan and same lot size, built in the same year, can sometimes differ in price by $50,000!! The difference in price may stem from interior upgrades, whereas one home may be fully upgraded with high-end finishings, and a property that looks the same from the outside has standard builder-grade finishings on the inside. Experienced agents will leverage their resources, ask questions of other agents about recently sold properties in the area, apply knowledge of recently toured similar properties, and compare interior pictures from other listing sites. All of this information helps the agent provide insight to the client on a home's value so that it will be "priced to sell."

An agent should think like an appraiser when valuing a home. An appraiser will determine an appraised value of the home that will be used to justify the amount being financed by the buyer. Appraisers will primarily use comparable sales in their analysis.

It is important to realize that an appraiser does not automatically add the total cost of upgrades spent by the homeowner into the total appraised home value. For example, if a seller spent $12,000 remodeling the kitchen, the appraiser will not automatically add $12,000 to the total appraised home value. Yes, there is absolutely a benefit to remodeling your kitchen in order to help sell your home; however, it might not add an equally proportionate value to the home. Why? Because trends and preferred styles change over time and with each individual buyer.

One strategy to help the home appraise at its highest is to consult with the seller and identify all updates made to the home, specifically recording the year and cost for each change, and presenting this list to the appraiser. This can help maximize the value an appraiser establishes.

It's important as a seller to view your home as a buyer would and make the impressions as positive and simple as possible. To attract buyers your home should appear as open, clean, fresh, and neutral as possible. Trends and preferred styles change over time and in many cases a minimal improvement to update a property prior to putting it on the market will make a big difference for buyers viewing the property online or in person. If they see something they really like they will have a favorable reaction and remember the home.

Marketability

Home improvements, both large and small, can drastically change the marketability of a home, and ultimately affect the final sale price.

Once a homeowner is emotionally and financially ready to sell their home, it might not be in proper condition to show to prospective buyers. Don't scramble to get your home in its best condition for attracting buyers. Plan and prepare ahead of time with the help of a knowledgeable agent for attracting buyers.

It can be difficult for buyers that walk through a home to look past wallpaper that might not be their style, and be able to envision themselves in the space. In most cases small cosmetic changes such as a fresh coat of paint or a professional carpet cleaning can make a huge difference to a potential buyer.

Instead of being discouraged by a certain paint color in the dining room, they leave the viewing appointment envisioning themselves or their family creating memories around the dinner table.

Go ahead and paint the wall a neutral color, fix a broken light fixture, as well as pull weeds and re-plant a few flowers in the garden. If buyers see things that are broken or that aren't maintained, then they will automatically eliminate the property from their list. Take action on maintenance items according to your budget, so that the home looks well maintained and cared for.

One of the most important aspects of preparing your home to sell is de-cluttering—simplifying the space in which you live. Take most of the small personal items and valuables off of walls, mantles, and shelves and store them away while your home is on the market. If needed, move select furniture pieces to the garage so the home looks spacious and not too busy. Sometimes just removing a chair in the living room or dresser in the bedroom can change a home from looking cluttered and overwhelming to looking spacious and inviting. Allow buyers to walk through the rooms and imagine their own furniture, pictures, and style throughout the home.

Tools to Sell

Exposing your home to the maximum amount of qualified buyers is key to selling your Southern California home at the best price. North San Diego County is a very desirable place to live, and as a result, property values are much higher in San Diego than the national average, especially along the coast.

There are many people that dream of living near the beach in California, and in addition to potential buyers who already live in North County, potential buyers also come from Los Angeles, the Inland Empire, and other areas in the U.S. and Canada who wish to escape cold winter weather.

One tool that is an effective way to help sell a property is an open house just for local agents. They often have a list of buyers waiting for a specific type of property, and by visiting the property they may realize that the home is an ideal fit for one of their clients. Other tools include flyers and electronic newsletters distributed to my network of agents, both here in the area, and across the country.

Today, most buyers are viewing available properties online, so Internet exposure is critical. Listings posted to our Multiple Listing Service (MLS) are directly connected to Realtor.com and Zillow.com, and are syndicated to many other online sites. A detailed property description and high-quality photographs are crucial to maximizing Internet exposure. Because the Internet is such a visual medium, quality photography can sometimes be the determining factor in a successful sale by simply getting the right buyer in the door to see the home.

By accessing my relationships with highly rated photographers, the pictures on my listings are always top-notch. De-clutter before the photo-shoot to create attractive and inviting pictures. Professional photographers will shoot the interiors and exterior in the best light and from the best angles to enhance the appearance for viewing. Buyers will make their most critical judgments in just a few seconds and we want them to be immediately wowed with what they see. Many times they will make their initial decision just based on the pictures before even reading the description.

For example, I found a property for a potential buyer that matched up well with their home criteria; however, the online pictures were so horrible that I doubted I should even put the house on the list to tour. We ultimately viewed the property, and surprisingly, it was a beautiful home, much better than the pictures portrayed. It was in great condition and was a perfect fit. The online presentation probably detracted the majority of potential buyers, so our client was able to negotiate and buy the property without much, if any, competition.

Online videos are also effective, since a video is more likely to be viewed, helping potential buyers visualize the home better than by just reading a description. Videos are easily shareable via social media, helping to spread the word quickly.

What Sellers Are Saying

"Paul was great to work with. We used Paul's services for two transactions and both were great experiences. Paul communicated great and his knowledge of the market was very impressive. I would recommend Paul to anyone looking to buy or sell a home."

"Paul worked with us in real time. We let him know what we were looking for and the general area that we liked. He sent us homes and lots that fit our description. When our dream home became available he immediately helped us to write up a family profile and then met with the seller and their agent to get us in front of them even before the first open house. The deal was done that day and the house became ours. He then helped us set a price on our home and had it sold within two weeks of it's listing. He is a great real estate agent with developer/contractor knowledge and is honest and forthright. He even closed our deal with a nice dinner with he and his wife. A family man with high moral integrity and values. We remain good friends to this day."

"Paul was great to work with. His local knowledge and expertise helped us sell our house in under a week! Paul always kept us informed and answered questions quickly. Paul was very professional and honest. I consider him the best and easiest Realtor to work with. I have recommended him to several friends and family members and he has brought that same level of professionalism each time. I will continue to recommend him to anyone looking to sell their home."

Buying Your Coastal North County Home

Selecting an agent is the first step in one of the most important decisions you will make in life—buying a home. And selecting the right agent is the most important part of the home buying process! What? – Selecting the right agent is more important than selecting the right house? YES! A good agent will do more than just show you properties and write up a purchase contract. An experienced agent will be your advocate, leveraging relationships from start to finish to successfully complete the transaction. An agents' job is not finished once an offer is accepted; it continues until you happily walk through the front door.

The strength of a real estate market fluctuates over time, and when a real estate market is "hot," desirable homes for sale often receive multiple offers shortly after being listed. A potential buyer must be prepared to act quickly to avoid missing out on the right home. Start working with an experienced agent as soon as you are contemplating buying a home to help you get fully prepared.

The right agent will lead you to the right house with care and attention, apply knowledge gained from experience to help your offer get accepted, and finally, help you navigate through the contract period for a successful purchase close. Just like the popular song sung by recording artist Stevie Wonder says, "Signed, Sealed, Delivered, I'm Yours," let's use similar terms to illustrate how important the right agent is to helping you achieve your homeownership goals: find, sign, deliver.

Find

An agent's foremost responsibility is to develop a relationship with clients that will help the agent understand their needs and be able to guide them to the right home. An effective agent can often help clients realize when they've found the right home before they even realize it themselves. Then, the agent should act as your advocate throughout the process.

Most buyers start their search for a home by looking online. It's easy to see a description and pictures of the property as well as the identity of the listing agent. It may be tempting to just make an offer through the listing agent; however, since the listing agent is working for, and has a fiduciary responsibility to the sellers, buyers are generally recommended to work with their own agent that will fairly represent them in negotiations. There is no cost to the buyer, and, in fact, the commission for the buyer's side comes from the seller. By having their own agent, buyers can be confident that someone is looking out for their best interests, educating on property values, and negotiating on their behalf. Buyers' agents also may have exposure to more available properties than may be listed online and can guide buyers to selecting a property that best suits their needs.

Finding the right home can seem overwhelming. Start by making a flexible wish list and establishing your budget.

Wish lists that are not flexible can often foster unrealistic expectations when looking for a home. In my experience of helping clients buy a home, very few homes have ever met every wish list item. Prioritize your wish list so that you know what aspects of a home are a "must-have" and which aspects are negotiable.

Establishing a budget creates realistic parameters that will guide your home search. Your budget should be determined by the loan value for which you can qualify, if you intend to pay for a home with a loan.

Without an established budget, buyers may be setting themselves up for disappointment by looking at homes outside their price range, then become discouraged when they start looking at homes within their more realistic budget and discover that the homes aren't as desirable. It can be really tough to take your sights down to less expensive properties when you've had expectations of purchasing a higher priced home.

The process of establishing your budget should be determined through prequalification. Prequalifying for a loan serves two purposes; one, to help you establish your budget, and two, to strengthen your offer once you find the right home.

In today's market, offers are not even being considered without a pre-approval letter from a lender or proof of funds in the case of a cash purchase. It's an active market and sellers are not willing to take a property off of the market when they are unsure if a buyer will qualify for financing.

The worst thing that happens to some buyers is that they are looking online for a few months, they make a decision to move to a new home, and they find their dream home listed online. They call me to work with them and the first question I ask is if they have their financing lined up. Typically the answer is "no." Unfortunately in this case their dream home may be gone by the time they meet with a lender and get their pre-approval, a process that typically takes up to two weeks. Like most active agents, I have a list of preferred lenders that can quickly underwrite and provide a pre-approval, assuming the buyer is diligent in providing all of the required documentation.

When a potential buyer submits an offer to buy a home accompanied with a prequalification letter, the seller's agent can feel confident that the contract period will go more smoothly.

Sign

You've found the home of your dreams but it's not yours yet. You want to make an offer and sign the deal, but what if it's not accepted. What terms, other than highest price, can help you differentiate your offer from a competitor? Working with a knowledgeable and experienced agent with relationships throughout the industry will help increase your chances that an offer is accepted. For example, I routinely encourage my clients to submit an offer quickly, without hesitation; advise them on what price will be most competitive, without over paying; and consult them on other terms that will result in an accepted offer.

When working with a buyer, agents should apply their knowledge of comparable properties, and other information such as upgrades and improvements that add value to a home, in order to educate the client on market value and the right price to include in the offer. A potential buyer should make a fair offer that will appease both the seller and the potential buyer—an offer that will be considered by the seller, but is not overpriced.

Submitting an offer is often an emotional decision and in a "hot" market, can often lead to a competitive situation where there are multiple offers on the same house. In a multiple counter offer situation, the lender's appraisal will generally work to protect against over-paying for a home.

Many buyers wonder how a home's appraisal affects the loan value. Most negotiated and accepted offers have a contingency on the lender's appraisal, requiring that the appraised value of the home meet or exceed the negotiated price. In rare instances, the appraised value of the home is lower than the negotiated price. This can happen, for example, when a buyer believes the negotiated price is fair, but the property may be over-improved to the extent that the appraiser can't apply enough value in the upgrades and improvements to justify the price.

When a home appraises lower than the negotiated contract price it negatively affects the home's loan-to-value ratio. For example, if a buyer is qualified for an 80% conventional loan, then the lender will loan up to 80% of the property's value based on the appraised price, not the negotiated contract price. The buyer typically has to make up the difference in price with cash.

To avoid paying the difference in cash, the buyer can specify in its purchase contract that they won't pay more than the appraised value. As a result, the seller must decide whether or not to seek another buyer and risk accepting an offer at an even lower sales price.

Another potential outcome of a low appraised home value is to stay committed to the original contract and add more cash into the deal to meet the lender's guidelines. Or, make an effort to re-negotiate the price by meeting the seller in the middle of the difference in price. There is little risk in trying to re-negotiate because the typical contract has protection for the buyers so they're not locked in if the appraisal is less than the price.

Deliver

Once an offer is signed, an agent has 30-45 days, depending on the contract, to close the deal and deliver the keys. An experienced agent will help the client navigate the contract period by advising on each step of the process. This will include effective communication, regularly working with the lender and selling agent; working through the list of repairs, if any, after an inspection; and working through the appraisal process.

Buyers should know what they are buying, so purchase contracts include a contingency for performing inspections and obtaining acceptable inspection results. Most agents have relationships with qualified inspectors that can determine the condition of the structure, mechanical and electrical systems, and appliances. The inspector is looking out for the best interests of the buyer as well as the agent to make sure the buyer has a good experience with their purchase, knowing that the property has been well maintained.

Termites are a risk factor in the region, so a termite inspection is always critical to make sure the home has been treated on a regular basis and there is not damage that needs to be repaired. If the inspector finds potential issues with mechanical or electrical systems, bringing in a contractor specializing in the particular system in question is recommended to check the situation in detail.

What Buyers Are Saying

"Paul is a professional, knowledgeable, responsive, easy-going, assertive, energetic and proficient agent. My husband and I consider him a superlative agent, in that he listens to your needs and wants, provides guidance without his commission as his primary concern, has many resources and much experience on which to draw to assist with your real estate search, purchase, repair and maintenance.
Paul treats each customer personally and as a good friend; he will not let you down. We highly recommend Paul, and will work with him again should we purchase another home in the future."

"Paul was the ultimate professional and extremely helpful during our home finding process. He took time to learn the needs of our family and tailored our search accordingly. He was always flexible and showed us several homes throughout North County. His extensive knowledge of the area was instrumental in helping us choose the right neighborhood for our family. He helped us find the perfect home and his guidance made the purchasing process a smooth and positive experience. Unlike other Realtors, our relationship with Paul did not end once he found us a home. After purchasing our home, we decided to add a new stairway and loft to create more space for our family. As we had no prior experience in home construction projects, Paul

helped us step-by-step through the difficult process. His vast network of trusted contractors allowed us to complete a quality project at a great price. Paul truly went above and beyond to make sure that our family would be happy. Paul treated us like family and it is plain to see that he genuinely cares for people and wants to serve others. We love our home and are extremely grateful for the exceptional service he provided. We highly recommend Paul to anyone searching for a Realtor."

"Paul, is without a doubt, the best real estate agent I have ever dealt with. He had our family's best interest in mind throughout our buying process. He listened to what our needs were. He made recommendations without ever imposing. And he followed up with us consistently both during the process of finding a home, and once we found the home. He continues to be a great resource even after we have closed. I would recommend him to anyone looking for a home in North County San Diego."

Finding the Right Agent for You

Find an agent who is most familiar with your desired location. Some real estate agents like to work throughout all of San Diego County to stay diversified across the geographic area and to stay familiar with the different cities and towns, climates, lifestyle opportunities, and property values. Other real estate agents like to specialize in more concentrated areas. I believe localized knowledge and experience is superior when buyers and sellers are looking for someone to represent them in their real estate transactions.

One benefit to selecting an agent who specializes in a clients' desired location is the relationships that agent has developed among other associates in the specific area that will help the client successfully complete a transaction. For example, I live in the coastal area of North San Diego County and most of my activity is in the same area. Because I have completed more than 60 transactions in North County within the last five years, I have the contacts, established relationships, and resources to help my clients buy or sell their home without a learning curve. Since North County is my neighborhood, I know other agents who are on the opposite side of the transaction and, because of the established working relationship, we look forward to working together again. My local knowledge also benefits my clients because I work, play, and socialize in the very neighborhoods they are interested in and I can point them to the areas that will be a best match.

One caution: beware of agents who sell themselves as the "biggest and best," then hand you off to a team member who is inexperienced. Work to ensure the agent is going to be available and is going to personally work with you on all aspects of the process.

Purchasing or selling a home is one of the largest transactions an individual or family will make. Whether buyer or seller, it's important to feel comfortable with an agent you are trusting to provide advice throughout the process; one that you feel is honest and ethical and that is going to look out for your best interests.

The North County Coastal Area

The San Diego North County coast is one of the most attractive areas of the entire world. The climate is second to none in the United States and there are year-round outdoor activities for every taste nearby. You can live near the beach and have the true California lifestyle.

Coastal North County San Diego boasts mild winters, with access to excellent ski resorts only a three-hour drive away. Local downtown centers dot the coastline, each with their own unique small-village character, yet we are only about 25 to 35 miles to a true metropolitan city, downtown San Diego, "America's Finest City." San Diego County offers both large land parcels just a few minutes inland from the beach, as well as a laidback lifestyle on the coast. The coastal area has it all and is a great place to live.

About Paul Jacinto

Paul Jacinto is an eleven-year seasoned Real Estate Broker and Agent, who is dedicated to client satisfaction and building solid relationships. Upon founding The Harding Realty Team, Paul immediately applied specialized knowledge of the San Diego and Riverside County areas to assist clients with successful purchases and sales of properties ranging in value from $275,000 to $12,000,000. He applies experience, having completed more than 100 million dollars in real estate transactions to assist clients throughout all of Southern California.

Because Paul is deeply familiar with North County San Diego, he can quickly evaluate properties that will best fit his clients' needs, keeping in mind style, budget, family size, or investment return. Relationships drive his core business model. By focusing on relationships with clients, buyers, sellers, and other agents, the Harding Realty Team has quickly expanded its business through word-of-mouth and repeat transactions as a result of happy clients and associates who prove that the best compliment for a job well done is a referral.

Founded in 2006, Harding Realty team's Principals, Agents, and Advisers bring more than a combined 65 years of experience including expertise in Brokerage, Property Management, and Land Development. The Harding Realty Team, affiliated with Keller Williams in Carlsbad, represents clients throughout all of Southern California, with specialized experience in coastal North San Diego County.

For more information about Paul Jacinto and the Harding Realty Team, visit www.HardingRealtyInc.com.

Real Estate Transactions for Seniors

By Ron Greenwald and Patti Gerke

Introduction

Most seniors prefer to stay in their homes as long as possible, but sometimes a move becomes necessary due to health, mobility or financial challenges. Some active seniors decide to move as they age, right-sizing to a more appropriate home or relocating to a senior residential community. Whatever the reason for a move and home sale, it can be an overwhelming experience for those involved. There are so many atypical considerations involved such as preparing the home for sale, finding a new home, selling or donating furnishing and personal possessions, and dealing with a variety of professional advisors. Although Ron Greenwald and Patti Gerke help a range of real estate buyers and sellers in the greater San Diego County area, they specialize in assisting seniors and their families through the sale of a home by serving as a single point of contact for a series of comprehensive services. They are sensitive to the needs of their clients and have the patience and empathy to help clients through the emotional experience of moving.

Ron has a background in finance, accounting and real estate. He was in the mortgage origination business for a decade before transitioning to real estate sales. As he was getting involved in real estate, he recognized the growing senior demographic and the need for a service level beyond the typical listing and marketing of properties. He concluded that specialized knowledge was required and started meeting with and was mentored by professional private fiduciaries, estate and trust attorneys, and other professionals that typically advise seniors or manage their affairs to understand how to best serve this growing market in a professional manner. Over the years, he has gained a reputation among professional advisors as one of the top real estate agents in the area when it comes to helping seniors and their family members with their real estate transactions.

Patti worked in the corporate world in marketing and sales management roles for medical device companies, as well as in marketing consulting prior to becoming a professional Realtor for 16+ years. Her desire to help seniors was based on her personal 12-year journey helping her parents through years of declining health issues and multiple housing transitions. While helping her parents, one parent suffering from multiple strokes, and the other parent suffering from vascular dementia, Patti experienced the draining physical and emotional challenges of family confusion and vulnerability. She watched her parents' health decline while their need for housing options, caregiving, and support grew each day. Starting with the first step of downsizing their home and then to independent living, assisted living, in and out of skilled nursing, board and care, and Alzheimer's care, she has lived it all! After learning the lessons of caring and fighting for one's parents through years of constant vigilance, Patti made it her mission to help and share with others her knowledge and insights. With each passing day more and more families are facing the challenge of aging parents and loved ones. Patti is there with empathy and has become a reliable professional assisting seniors, their family members, and their trusted advisors.

In this chapter, Ron Greenwald and Patti Gerke provide their insight for seniors and their families when considering a move that includes a real estate transaction.

Considerations for Real Estate Transactions for Seniors

Determining Lifestyle Goals When Considering a Move

For younger families, a real estate transaction is mostly an uplifting, positive experience where they're looking forward to moving to a new home. It may be from a condo to a single-family residence or to a larger house because they have more children. For most seniors it's not necessarily an upbeat situation. A move could be necessary due to mobility or health concerns and many times the move is from a property where the older adults raised their family and lived for decades creating lifelong cherished memories. It is a highly emotional time.

When a senior is starting to think about a move they should consider any physical limitations and their lifestyle goals for the next several years. Sometimes they are healthy and active and just don't want to continue to maintain a large property, so they want to right-size their house. Many have some mobility limitations and are having trouble with stairs in their home. Others foresee the need to move to retirement community or an assisted-living apartment.

If the objective is to move to an appropriate single-family house, a house with a single floor is generally going to be one of the requirements, even if there are no current mobility limitations. An important point is that in the developed coastal areas of California, land is very expensive, particularly in San Diego County. Lots are therefore quite small along the coast and there are not many houses with a single floor. It's a different situation inland and in fact lot sizes can be quite a bit larger, necessitating more landscape maintenance. The topography also differs greatly from coast to inland where 10 miles inland from the coast can mean 15 degrees difference in temperature.

An option for some people, especially for those that are still very active, is a 55+ community. Residents in these communities are not all necessarily retired. These communities are generally more affordable and there are usually more single-story homes. In the majority of these communities, the range of activities to spur physical and mental exercise is extensive. Many communities will have rec rooms, swimming pool(s), ballrooms, and much more. If they need some assistance, they may want to consider communities where there are progressive care living options, versus a community that's just for independent living. Within these communities, they may need to change apartments, but they don't have to change communities and lose their friends and feel like they have to start all over again. With any potential move to a senior community, the older adult should visit all the potential communities, talk with the residents, meet with the staff, make unannounced visits to get a sense of the atmosphere and mood, and most of all, enjoy their cuisine.

Even if one is thinking about moving closer to their family members, remember that those relatives have their lives to lead. To have a successful move to a senior community, you will want to embrace both the activities and your immediate neighbors while giving appropriate space to your family members. Ask yourself the question, would you enjoy living in this community if the family member(s) were not in the immediate vicinity?

Then, obviously, there is the financial aspect of what the senior can afford. There are many different options and business models for the various senior living communities in your neighborhood—living arrangements, amenities, levels of care, low rise vs. high rise, for profit, not-for-profit entities, dining experiences, and so much more. From the board and care with 6 to 8 residents, to a continuing care retirement community serving hundreds of residents, with everything in between, you will need a spreadsheet to make sure you can compare and contrast the pluses and minuses that are important to you. What is the real cost going to be each month? For example, when a resident of a community requires more care and seeks assistance, what is the cost per month to administer the activities of daily living?

It's a Process and It's Going to Take Time

In our experience, from the time we get introduced to a senior who is starting to explore their housing options, to the time they make a change in their living arrangement, it may be 3 to 5 years. In general, the senior is not thrilled with the prospect of a move. They may not want to deal with the thought of what is an overwhelming decision. The result is a delay in the decision making process. The impact of procrastination is often a home with deferred maintenance. When we talk to families concerned for their aging parent(s), we spend quite a bit of time on the issue of making sure that while one ages in their home, it is as safe and sound as possible.

When aging adults have been living in their home for a significant length of time, there are going to be emotional ties to the real and the personal property. Even their children may not want their parents to leave due to their fond memories of growing up in the home. Assuming a change in housing is a foregone conclusion in the next year, 3 years, 5 years, what is most important to the senior's quality of life? Not to fall into depression, but how do we do that? We can try to make it an empowering process. The senior's perspective may change from resistance to embracing a possible housing change. How is that achieved? It takes a lot of listening and understanding. Many times, 3rd party professionals who specialize in this specific need are hired to assist all the family members involved. One very simple task may be to encourage an aging adult to give away their personal treasures while they are alive. Giving is joyous. When an aging adult sees the impact of giving their lifelong treasures to a grandchild, a charity, a library, or other loved ones, it is a great starting point to turn a somber thought into a celebration.

It's never too early to start talking about options and getting advice on an eventual move. Getting a home ready for sale can be a burden, especially if trying to get it ready in 30 to 60 days. We can suggest some of the hot buttons that can be started to compartmentalize the projects. What to do with all the "stuff" is always a number 1 or 2 question and concern. Whether you are 20 or 90 years of age, nobody is efficient and effective when it is all thrown at you at once. Therefore, the goal is to try to avoid the state of emergency move. The one when Mom or Dad has fallen, then moved from the hospital to a skilled nursing facility, and Doctor's order is to not allow the aging adult to move back home. What then?

<u>Legal Considerations</u>

The information below is intended to provide a general overview of some of the possible considerations. This content is not intended to be providing any legal, financial, or tax planning advice. Readers should consult with their own attorney, financial advisor, tax advisor, and related consultants in their state when considering a real estate transaction.

Selling real estate has a number of legal and tax implications and that is especially true with properties owned by seniors or an estate. One important factor relates to the ability of a senior property owner to conduct their business affairs.

If the seller is deemed to not be competent there are many legal implications for a real estate agent representing them as well as for a buyer. Our experience is that if we are concerned that our client has some limitations, we immediately seek the advice of those professional advisors that work with the client such as estate planning attorney, financial advisor, and even the physician. We, also, seek to talk to the prospective client's family members. We have to do this with the permission and consent of the client, who is seeking our real estate services.

If a parent does have cognitive impairment, a frequent observation is that the children are not well informed on the paperwork that is necessary to legally provide them the authority to sell their parents' real estate. They may think that with a power of attorney they have the legal right to sign and to sell their parent's home. If the home is in a trust and the parents have not resigned as trustees, the children do not have that right. We're not attorneys and we're not going to make the final call, but we always advise the children to check with an attorney to make sure all of the necessary legal documents are in place.

Selling the real property of a deceased person has many legal implications as well. Each state has specific laws in regards to selling real estate; was the real estate properly titled in the name of a trust or does it pass to the heirs through a will? If the home passes to the heirs other than a spouse and is not titled in the name of the trust, the details of the estate's assets may be exposed to the rules of a probate court proceeding. The full implications of time and money when going through probate proceedings are beyond the scope of this book.

If the real estate is properly titled in a trust, the successor trustee has a key decision to make before selling the home. The main decision point is to sell the home "as is," or make updates to the home to maximize its selling price. Are there any funds within the trust to make improvements to the home to get it ready for sale? What is the projected rate of return to any improvements made to the home prior to listing for sale?

Another component of selling a home by a successor trustee or an estate executor is the family dynamics. After the passing of a parent and loved one, the rivalry bubbling beneath the surface between siblings can rear its ugly head and create challenges when looking to distribute personal property and sell the real estate.

The overriding themes of this section are that each state has their own rules covering the subject of selling real estate of a deceased relative and proper and effective estate planning, well in advance of a crisis, is vital to family legacy and harmony.

Personal Property

One of the common overwhelming tasks our clients deal with—whether the senior is still living or has passed away—is deciding what to do with all of their personal property. Our seniors, the "Greatest Generation," were raised during the Great Depression and many had little in the way of possessions. After World War II, the economic revival and wealth creation of the general population resulted in accumulation of possessions, which are very important to their sense of accomplishment and legacy. Today's baby boomers, their children, and their children's children have shown little interest in inheriting the possessions of those born prior to 1945.-

If our senior client has lived in the home for a very long time, dealing with all of the "stuff" acquired over a lifetime can be paralyzing. Those possessions that have meant so much to them are hard to give up, but for the most part they will be moving to a smaller space so there won't be room for everything. There is also a concern for the children's attachment to certain items that may have minimal financial value but very high sentimental value. We strongly suggest that they don't dispose of anything until the children, grandchildren, and all family members have a chance to really look through the house and see what means something to them. As we noted previously, the way the distribution of the personal property is handled can be the event that dictates when and if the real property can be sold.

One of the biggest misconceptions is the value of the possessions in the house, including furniture. Collectibles, as example Hummel figurines, were very popular in past decades, but with tastes changing, many such collectible items today are valued at a very small fraction of their original cost. Sterling silver flatware has declined in popularity, as younger people don't want to spend the time polishing it. A lot of people inheriting sterling silver just watch the market price for silver, looking for a good time to liquidate it to be melted down.

Preparing the Home for Sale

No matter what the situation is, the number one goal in selling a house is obtaining top dollar and selling in the shortest amount of time. Whether we are working with a senior, the children, or a fiduciary, this is always the top priority with respect to the real property. With many of the properties we get involved with, the senior has been living in the home for a long time and more often than not, there is deferred maintenance and a lack of updates to the home. They may have been living with these issues for a long time and they just have not been a priority.

The key is to make the property presentable; otherwise selling it for top dollar is a real challenge. It's amazing what paint and new carpeting can do to the appearance. Sometimes there is an attachment to certain out-of-date features or decorating that might be an obstacle for a sale. As an example, they may have some very outdated wallpaper and a small investment in updating the wallpaper or removing the wallpaper and painting can make a big difference in attracting buyers. It can take some time for the owner to be convinced of the need for making some of these minor decorating changes, so we will sometimes discuss this topic with the children or the client's other advisors. When they hear the same recommendation from a number of people they trust, they are more likely to come around to the same view in order to maximize the sales amount.

Even though the property may not be fully updated, we want there to be some sizzle. We think it is beneficial to stage a home so that any buyer who comes in can see the potentially of what the home could be, even if it's a 50, 60, 70-year-old home that's not been updated in recent times.

Pricing the Property

Properly pricing the property for sale is one of the keys to selling it in a reasonable time and actually can result in a higher price than if the property hits the market at an unrealistically high price. There is a lot of information available online about estimated values, but these are based on computer algorithms where there is no data about the actual conditions in the house. This can lead to a misconception about the actual value and what buyers will be willing to pay. Many times the estimated values are too high, especially when the home has not been updated and may not be comparable to others in the neighborhood. The seller may note that there has been some major remodeling done in the house, such as a complete kitchen update. The important point is how long ago was the work done and does it match current trends? If a kitchen was remodeled 20 years ago, it's certainly not going to present as a modern update. These points are generally sensitive and an honest conversation is important to not offend anyone involved in the process.

It's important to have a good set of comparable sales data for the area, showing exact sales information over the past 6 to 12 months, comparing the property to other most similar properties. This provides a realistic picture and we recommend pricing at the market value, not higher. Sometimes the client will want to price higher than recommended and we'll go along with the understanding that we give it two weeks and then have another frank discussion. We can always start a little high, but the truth is the market will tell us within the first two weeks whether we're right or not, because if you're too high, you won't even get any showings. If you're just a little bit high you'll get showings and no offers, and if you're priced right you'll get showings and you'll get offers.

Team Approach

A team approach is generally recommended to assist in making the appropriate and correct decisions relating to a move. Family members are important due to emotional concerns, estate planning, and disposition of personal possessions. The financial planner should be involved if they are working with one. A CPA should be consulted to determine if there are capital gains tax concerns. Their estate-planning attorney should be involved to make sure the contemplated transaction is being made in accordance with the estate or trust. Some seniors have a professional private fiduciary or bank trust officer to manage their financial affairs. And, of course when there is a home sale as part of the move, a real estate professional should be part of the team and be involved as early as possible to help provide options related to the current property intended sale.

Selecting a Real Estate Professional

Helping seniors or estates in selling a property is a very specialized segment of the real estate sales profession. Due to the typical complexities, and variety of advisors involved in most of these transactions, specific knowledge and experience in serving seniors and estates is important. Agents that have the knowledge and experience will typically have relationships with professional private fiduciaries, bank trust officers, estate planning attorneys, financial planners, accountants, and others that work to bring product and services to our seniors.

As mentioned above, a senior's decision-making process to move is frequently drawn out over time and the agent should be patient in working with such a client. They need to find someone who's sensitive to their needs and understanding of their situation, versus someone who's just there to take a listing. It's generally not going to be a listing meeting and a rapid decision to list, like with most transactions. It's important to select an agent that will make them comfortable, will maintain a high level of communications with all involved parties, and one that will treat the client the same way they would treat their own parents and family.

The agent should also be familiar with the legal aspects noted; otherwise a listing agreement may not even be valid if the person signing it does not have the legal capacity to sign such a document.

What Clients and Professionals Are Saying

"Forgive my delay in offering thanks for your handling of our house sale. I'm still feeling a little giddy with the extra dollars in my life. Your administration of this project has been completely professional from the get-go. Not only did you extend our family every courtesy, you patiently took us through the estate process with an eye towards explaining the unknowns and answering our endless questions. Such extra depth in client services seems sadly to have become real rarity in our culture. Your attitude helped my siblings and me to navigate a potentially emotional adventure with a minimum of fear and anxiety. Please receive my thanks and gratitude for your skill and consideration. I would not hesitate to seek your representation in any future transaction, nor would I hesitate to endorse your involvement to anyone asking my opinion. If you're not careful, you're going to give realty brokers a good name!"

- Matthew M.

"If any one has a case with residential real estate in the San Diego area, you should give Ron Greenwald a call. He handled a property for one of my cases exceptionally well. He was efficient! The property had some issues and I really appreciated the level of service Ron and his staff provided.

Together we priced this home in the midst of the major market slowdown that was occurring and he really helped to get the home on the market just before the holidays. It sold at higher than list price with 15 back-up offers. I expected to have to sit on this house for a few months, but we were able to get it sold quickly and for a great price! If anyone is a member of the Southern California PFAC listserv, please re-post so the fiduciaries in that area know what a wonderful job Ron did for us."

- Loren Acuna, Ace Fiduciary Group

"Patti, I just want to thank you for all your hard work and excellent service you provided towards the sale of my sister's condo in San Marcos. I so much appreciate your professionalism and willingness to work with me being out of state, as well as your patience during the restoration of my sister Cynthia's condo, which was a several month process.

I also thank your husband for all the time and effort he provided to physically make the repairs to my sister's place, and in such a timely fashion. All your efforts were far and beyond any Realtor I have ever worked with before and I will certainly keep you in mind if I need a Realtor in the Escondido area in the future."

- Dr. Stephen P., M.D.

"Nancy and I are writing this on be half of Patti and Ron. Their effort, empathy, and hard work allowed my wife Nancy to fulfill her role as successor trustee on behalf of her mother's wishes. We were referred to Patti and Ron by a manager for a senior living community. Although my mother-in-law did not move to this particular community, we were pleased to interview Patti and Ron as potential listing agents for the home and two vacant adjoining lots.

Nancy and I quickly determined that Patti and Ron are very knowledgeable. They excel a working with families and successor trustees, communicating with attorneys, and most of all, getting top dollar. In spite of the home's deferred maintenance, we were well compensated for both the home and two vacant buildable lots. In addition Patti and Ron contributed ideas, suggestions, and recommendations for specific situations which included how to deal with a family member who along with his extended family was living at the home that needed to be sold. Most of all, they kept in close, three-way communication with us and our attorney as we weaved through the legal process of being successor trustee of the estate.

Nancy and I highly recommend Patti and Ron for their commitment to superior service, going above and beyond, and being highly skilled at marketing and negotiations. Patti and Ron combine the forces of being superior relators with the sensitivity of working with seniors and/or their family members when it comes to sell the family home."

- Jon and Nancy P.

"The closing date of my Aunt's home, has come and gone, but I have not forgotten the awesome professionalism, expertise and friendship that was demonstrated by you and your associates. I could tell from the time we met that you understood the situation and knew exactly what direction we needed to meet our family's needs. Your knowledge of the market; the examples of recent home sales in the area; your unique marketing and pricing techniques and your honesty in our deliberations made this Realtor experience worth remembering. In addition, it really helps the client when you have the experiences and the connections of the San Diego senior communities, especially with someone like myself who was from Ohio and was trying to manage my Aunt's affairs.

A huge thanks to you and your staff for the opportunity to work with you. If you need a reference please do not hesitate to ask. I hope your new year greets you well personally and professionally."

- John M.

"During this time of giving special thanks my husband and I wanted you to know how thankful we are for the referral. Since we live in the Chicago area it was more then meaningful for us to feel secure in the people handling the sale of our friend's condo.

Ron laid the preliminary steps out via phone calls and emails and in just a very short time we were on our way. I felt we were treated in a friendly manner albeit most professional. It's nice to be treated as a functioning adult (although there is snow on the rooftop) rather than a non-entity. He does have a special touch with respect to the older person; but, then again, I'm sure you knew that......

We were most impressed when he called to thank us for choosing him to represent us in the sale. Without him the sale would not have happened so quickly. Hope does spring eternal. And, thank you!"

- Blanche and Ron O.

About Ron Greenwald and Patti Gerke

Ron Greenwald earned an MBA degree and worked in finance, accounting and mortgage origination prior to transitioning to real estate sales in 2009. He is the host of the Senior Stay or Go™ TV show and is a frequent speaker on the topic of "Compassionate Real Estate for Seniors."

Patti Gerke earned an MBA degree and worked in the medical device industry in a variety of sales and marketing management roles prior to getting involved in real estate sales in 2002. Having both real estate and personal experience working with ageing adults, she is a featured lecturer on the management of senior housing transitions.

She is also the co-host of the Senior Stay or Go™ TV show.

Ron and Patti help a range of real estate buyers and sellers in the greater San Diego County area, but they specialize in assisting seniors and their families through the sale of a home. They coordinate all aspects related to their clients' home sales, working with professional advisors such as professional private fiduciaries, trust and estate attorneys, financial advisors, accountants, and others. They have a TV show called, "Senior Stay or Go," which advocates and educates on behalf of seniors.

For more information on Ron Greenwald and Patti Gerke, visit http://www.GreenwaldGerke.com.

Buying and Selling Homes In North San Diego County

By Scott Voak

Introduction

Scott Voak started his career in sales and marketing in the high technology industry after earning a Bachelor's Degree in Electrical Engineering. He later earned an MBA and then ran a start-up company. Scott entered the real estate industry with a Southern California residential housing project developer as Vice President of Land Acquisitions.

Scott received a strong background in positioning and marketing homes while working with the development company. He decided to use his skills to help individual clients market their homes and has been doing that full time for over 15 years. Scott is the Managing Partner for Sotheby's International Realty's San Diego Inland Corridor office. He primarily helps sellers of executive and estate homes in the North County area with a primary focus within the boundary of the Poway Unified School District.

In this chapter Scott Voak provides insights for buyers and sellers in the North San Diego County area.

Selling Your North County Home

Positioning a home in the market is a fundamental key to receiving the best response from potential buyers and selling for the highest price. Most people are familiar with Zillow, which provides an estimate of property value; however, the value shown is based on an algorithm that does not take into consideration the actual differences among houses in the area. When valuing a home it's critical to review a number of factors that only an experienced agent with local knowledge can provide. Even the values of two very similar houses in the same neighborhood will be different because of a number of factors such as view, proximity to traffic noise, condition of the property, level of upgrades, and age of updates.

When you are ready to sell your home, preparing for sale is quite a bit different than living in it. It needs to appeal to the widest range of potential buyers, so you can get the maximum value from the sale in the shortest time. When buyers are looking at a home, they don't have a lot of vision if it doesn't immediately seem to suit their tastes. They are looking for instant gratification and generally won't consider a home that needs some changes. Even something as simple as a wall painted in a bright color that buyers find offensive may completely turn them off, even if it's a very simple and inexpensive change.

When I'm working with a seller, I walk through the home with an interior designer and staging company to determine the best way to present the home. We'll make a list of things that need to be done to get it ready for sale. This may include a number of small changes like painting dark walls a neutral color. The designer and staging company will advise on furniture placement and sometimes we will remove some of the furnishing to give the home an open, spacious look. Before presenting the home to buyers it needs to be clean and free of clutter. It should provide an image that it has been taken care of and well maintained. The yard needs to have some attention as well, as the first impression is made as the prospective buyer is walking from the street or driveway to the front door.

Our review includes a comparison of the condition of the home to other similar homes in the neighborhood, including how well it matches current buyer tastes. If the home hasn't been updated in several years it may need some improvements to attract buyers. If it's pretty obvious that most potential buyers would want to upgrade an important feature in the home or not even consider buying it, as is, it's going to be prudent to consider the upgrade before putting the home on the market. Another reason for doing this is that the amount of down payment required is a limiting factor for many buyers. They can make the monthly payments but funds are limited for a down payment. If they use their available funds for the down payment, money won't be available for upgrades immediately after the purchase. If a home is in need of $20,000 in upgrades, and the buyers are going to spend the money on upgrades after the purchase, they will have

$20,000 less for a down payment. Assuming a 20% down payment, this translates to $100,000 less they can pay for the home.

When considering any upgrades when selling, make sure your agent can provide a realistic assessment of the value-added, so you know that you will be getting a return on the investment. The improvements that I recommend often generate 3 to 4 times the cost, and in many cases payment can be delayed until escrow closes.

After the home has been prepared and staged, it's time to present the home to buyers. Today, most potential buyers start by searching on the Internet for homes; therefore, it's critical that the home is showcased well online. Buyers aren't even going to read the description about the home unless it looks visually appealing. Professional photos will show your home in the best possible light, make it pop online, and get buyers interested.

One thing we want to do in presenting your home is to make it appealing to buyers that are going to appreciate it. Another great tool we use today is a 3D Walkable Online Tour of the home. Buyers can virtually "walk" though the home and see everything and all the rooms in relationship to everything else, so they get a very good feel for the flow. This can create additional interest in the home, but it also can reduce in-person showings where the floor plan won't be working for the buyer. This helps cut down on showings where effort is taken to tidy up the home and the buyers walk in and immediately turn around to leave because the room arrangement doesn't work for them.

In relocation situations, one spouse may not be in town. The virtual tour helps the out-of-town spouse or partner visualize the flow of the home almost as well as being there in person.

In addition to the 3D virtual tours, video is another way to attract attention and let buyers appreciate the home while searching online. Although some homes are presented with virtual tours that simply pan pictures across the screen accompanied by bad music, a professional video with narration can really make the home shine. The agent can narrate over the video, describing the house and neighborhood in detail. In cases of truly unique properties, we can capture the owners talking about the details of the home. Videos often include aerial views to present the home within the neighborhood and show off the view.

One of our most important jobs as an agent is to market your home in such a way that every buyer interested in living in your area knows that your home is on the market. Then we need to bring those interested buyers through the house to try and convince one or more of them to make an offer. A good agent that understands marketing will give you a better opportunity of receiving multiple offers. Competition among buyers is the best way to get the highest offer possible. Extensive marketing through different channels will maximize the exposure of your home, but it costs a lot of money that many agents are not willing or able to spend.

In reality, we don't know specifically where the buyer for your home is going to find it, because people look for homes in a variety of ways. The important point is to present it in a wide range of media and channels so that it will get the most exposure. Too many agents give up on a marketing channel because they do it once or twice and it didn't work and they don't want to spend money on something that doesn't work. So, many agents selling 5-10 houses a year don't want to do multiple marketing channels because they haven't seen them work and they incorrectly assume they don't work. On the other hand, top producing agents that are closing say 30 to 50 home sales a year, are likely using a variety of marketing channels and they are seeing results with various methods. For example, a small full color ad in the Sunday paper could run $400. Most agents don't want to spend that so they say it doesn't work. I guarantee the Sunday paper will not work for you if you're not in the Sunday paper. The same can be said for most of the potential marketing channels. Find an agent that will invest in marketing through multiple channels.

In addition to local buyers looking to move to a larger or smaller house, San Diego County attracts buyers from around the United States as well as globally. There's an ideal climate and much of the county is just minutes from the ocean. It's a great area for almost every type of outdoor activity. A diverse economy with growing high-tech and biotech companies drives a large number of relocations to the area. In presenting your home it's important to be able to expose it to not just the local market, but to buyers across the U.S. and other countries as well. My approach includes local print advertising, digital marketing, and premium print and online media presented internationally that feature luxury or estate properties. The combination reaches a wide audience of likely buyers from around the world.

Something to be careful of is that some agents give an impression of marketing your house, but they are really promoting themselves. For example, Just Listed and Just Sold cards going to the neighbors do nothing to sell your home and are just promoting the agent. As long as you have a sign in the yard, your neighbors know your home is for sale. On the other hand, using the Internet and social media marketing to promote your home to likely buyers who are living in other parts of the country all focus on selling your home and not benefiting the agent, because people in other areas won't be listing a house with the agent.

One of my favorite strategies is to create a lot of excitement as the home is coming on the market. It's all focused on a release date open house when buyers and other agents can visit the home for the first time. The goal is to have several buyers walking through the home at the same time and observing the high level of interest. We try to create a fear in the minds of buyers that they might miss out on the opportunity and thus influence them to move rapidly and offer more than they might otherwise.

Once you have an offer, negotiations become a critical part of the process. A lot of buyers and sellers negotiate as part of their work, but it's very different than negotiating on a house. In business, you can generally count on people doing what makes sense for their business. Real estate transactions are emotional for the people involved and they can lose their minds over the simplest things. I've seen buyers walk over a $2,000 repair request, even after the agents offered to cover it. The buyer felt he had to "beat" the seller. The purchase contract can be 25 pages with all the addendums and you really need to understand how each clause affects you. An experienced agent can insert points into the contract during the initial negotiation that gives the seller leverage later in the process.

It's important for the negotiations to all be done in a professional manner. Most of the problems in real estate that I have had to fix for my agents are not buyer-seller issues; they are agent-agent ego issues. One agent made a mistake and is afraid to admit it to their client, so they get aggressive and you end up with a transaction in trouble and the buyer and seller don't know why.

The final point is to make sure the transaction gets closed. I see too many agents get into escrow and then pass the file to the transaction coordinator. The agent is responsible for making sure your home closes and should be monitoring everything and making sure the schedule and commitments are kept.

The agent a buyer is using is important to me as a sellers' agent because I want someone on the other side who has shown they can successfully close a transaction. If an agent writes an offer and they either work at a brokerage that I know to be a problem or they have little experience, I really push for my seller to pick a different offer, if we have multiple offers.

What Sellers Are Saying

"Scott is a real professional. We decided to sell our home late in the year and Scott stepped up to the plate and did an amazing job. He is very honest, dependable, and knowledgeable about the market. However, what my wife and I really appreciated was Scott's communication skills and style: He is very responsive, informative, and his recommendations are well thought through. He explained the issues with our timing and help set our expectations. Based on our situation and requirements, he put together the right marketing plan. He used all the tools at his disposal targeted for our type of home: brought in video professionals, magazine ads, open houses, and broker show cases. Additionally, Scott is well respected by his peers and has a great rapport with other agents. This too added to the amazing experience and added to the communication experience."

- emunar866

"Scott looks out for the best interest of the seller. He is very knowledgeable in the market, knows how to anticipate trends, and skilled in how to read buyers which is important in negotiation. His communication was prompt and he continuously kept me updated throughout the entire process. He also coordinated the repairs that needed to be done. I am very pleased with the service Scott provided and recommend him as an agent."

- Mellaa015

"Scott has provided us real estate advice and guidance for over four years now. He listed and sold our home prior to our Navy transfer four years ago. We greatly appreciate the fact that not only did we

have several offers within two weeks of the listing, but that after the sale was final and we closed, Scott maintained contact with us throughout our next tour. We were hopeful of returning to the San Diego area and it was of great importance to us to keep an eye on the market. When we did receive the good news we would be returning, Scott was the first person we contacted. He has helped us with both the transition of leaving and that of returning. We will have Scott represent us as we continue to search for our retirement home as well.

Scott's professionalism, knowledge of the area and attention to detail is second to none. We've worked with many real estate agents in other parts of the country and have found Scott to be the best. We feel that with each decision he's helped us make, he's kept our best interests first and foremost.

I would highly recommend Scott Voak and his team to anyone who may be buying, selling, renting their home or in need of a rental. He's always there for his clients!"

- helofam

"We've dealt with real estate agents in the past, but none with Scott's level of professionalism, expertise and responsiveness. Our transaction was complex in a difficult selling market; we received several offers after only one open house, secured a buyer and the sale was complete within a short period of time. He is very knowledgeable and explained every step of the process, kept us very well informed, and was patient with all of our questions and always got back to us right away. He is very familiar with the San Diego market, and especially the 4S Ranch area and we were well informed by him or his excellent staff every step of the way. He was also able to find us *a new place quickly that exceeded all of our expectations. We will definitely use him on our next purchase or sale."*

- sherio

Buying Your North County Home

Most homes for sale can be found on the Internet so most buyers begin their search for a home online. You can do a lot of research online, but it's difficult to get to know the details that can impact your long-term enjoyment of living in specific neighborhoods. An agent's knowledge of the local area is even more important for a buyer than for a seller, because a seller will know the neighborhood better than the agent. Some examples of local knowledge that will not be obvious with casual research include things like traffic patterns, there's a new principal in the school that's great (or maybe not so great); the leases in the local shopping center are expiring next year and the stores are staying (or going). A good buyer's agent will know all these details, which add value to a buyer.

As discussed earlier, the value shown on Zillow is not going to be accurate and the list price is probably not going to be correct either. An experienced buyer's agent will provide an analysis of the value but in the end you need to determine what the value of the property is to you, regardless of the list price. Then, work with your agent to try to get it for less than or equal to that number.

An observation I've made is that buyers tend to negotiate too hard on the price and walk away from homes they really want over numbers that seem big, but that over the long term, are actually small. I've seen buyers walk away on a $1million house over $10,000 when the house was perfect for their family. Now, $10,000 seems like a lot of money, but let's break it down:

- With 25% down, the cash increase is $2,500.
- $10,000 is 1% of the price. If the market is increasing 6% a year you're talking about 60 days of value increase. So, if the escrow closes in 45 days, you're paying market price for the house just 15 days early.
- If you are holding the home for 7 years, $10,0000 on the day you purchase is meaningless. If the market goes up 5% a year, the home will be worth over $1.4 million and if it goes down 5% a year it will be worth less than $700,000.

So, it's much more important "When" you buy than how good a "Deal" you get when you buy.

What Buyers Are Saying

"Scott Voak is a top-notch real estate professional and expert. His knowledge of the industry and area is well researched and so very helpful to San Diego home buyers and sellers. Scott and his team guided us through the home buying process in 4S Ranch with absolutely no problems. The support from Scott has not ended with the purchase of our home. Scott keeps us educated on market trends with his weekly industry updates and he provides a monthly home

valuation customized for our home and neighborhood. We give Voak Homes our highest recommendation!"

- kathyabullock

"Scott helped us buy and sell our house in Rancho Bernardo. We were first time home buyers and his excellent knowledge and patience helped us make a wise decision on selecting the best one for us. Scott also helped us sell the same home when we were relocating from San Diego. My husband and I think that he is the best agent in that area, and we highly recommend him."

- dnas78

Selecting an Agent

Whether buying or selling, your relationship with your agent is short but intense, so choose someone you feel comfortable working with. Buying or selling a home is one of the most significant financial transactions in life, so look for an agent that works full time and has the experience to guide you through to a successful closing. Sometimes the agent's experience level is not so obvious. For example, an agent can say, "I have sold 100 homes," meaning they have personally sold 100 homes. Or, an agent can say, "We have sold 100 homes." A consumer may assume "we" means the agent's team, but it could mean the entire company the agent works for. Agents are sales people, so they are trained to close. Unfortunately most agents focus on getting the listing, because once the listing is signed there is an 80% chance they are going to get paid. Once the house is listed, they lose focus; after all if the house sells for an extra $10,000 it's important to the seller, but it doesn't change the agent's income very much.

Ask enough questions to determine the level of experience and activity level. A successful agent will have many transactions each year and a good track record of satisfied clients. Look for online reviews and ask for a list of clients so you can check references. I discussed earlier about the importance of local knowledge. An agent that focuses on a more limited area rather than an expanded area or county-wide will naturally know a lot more about important details of individual neighborhoods and likely have a better sense of small differences in properties that drive value.

If you're selling, make sure the agent can show you marketing that they have done. Most agent fees are within a very small range – pick an agent who is going to invest a lot of that fee into marketing your home (rather than marketing themselves). Try to get a written marketing plan guaranteeing when and where your home will be marketed. Is the agent going to promote your home across a wide range of media, including online as well as print? Will the agent be investing in professional photography, videos, and a virtual 3D tour?

North San Diego County

North San Diego County is a diverse area, extending from Scripps Ranch on the south to Escondido on the north, and Rancho Santa Fe to the west and Poway to the east. Due to the strength of the school district, the area is very family focused and a bit more expensive than most other parts of San Diego.

Housing options range from 1-bedroom condominiums to 4-acre country club estates. It's common to see a young family move in just in time for their oldest to start kindergarten and move up within the community until their youngest graduates high school. After that they may start to look for a lifestyle move, either within the area or more toward the coast or downtown direction. It is not unusual for people to move 2-3 times within the school district before moving out.

A lot of the lifestyle surrounds kids and families. There are no nightclubs and just a few bars (there are several sports bars and brewery/restaurants). You can walk streets on Saturday and most people won't be home. It's Little League, dance, high school sports, band, etc.

No. County is very ethnically diverse but demographically oriented towards people with college degrees working in technology or running small companies.

About Scott Voak

Scott Voak is the Managing Partner for Sotheby's International Realty's San Diego Inland Corridor office. In addition to serving his own clients, as Managing Partner he trains other agents how to successfully market homes. Scott primarily works with sellers of executive and estate homes and his primary geographic focus is San Diego's inland corridor and more specifically the Poway Unified School District. He doesn't typically work with buyers because he can't get a seller the best price if he is also trying to get a buyer the lowest price. The exceptions are when a seller needs to buy or a friend wants to buy a home. He has been helping clients with their real estate transactions for over 15 years.

Scott earned a Bachelor's Degree in Electrical Engineering from Santa Clara University and worked in high-tech sales and marketing for 15 years and then obtained an MBA degree. He was the President of a start-up company and later entered the residential real estate development industry as Vice President of Land Acquisitions for a Southern California developer. While working in the development company, Scott learned how to develop residential housing projects as well as how to position and market homes successfully. This skill has transferred well to his real estate practice.

Scott is a multiple 5-Star Award Winner and in the course of his real estate practice he has been a real estate radio host, a real estate trainer, and guest speaker on the topic of real estate marketing.

In addition to excelling in real estate, Scott is actively involved as a member of the Board of Directors for both the Greater San Diego Boys & Girls Club and the Autism Society of San Diego, which he joined because his son, Zachary, has Fragile-X Syndrome, the leading genetic cause of autism and development delay. In his spare time, he is a competitive home brewer and has won regional and national awards for his beer. In his really spare time, Scott goes to the gym to work off the spare tire acquired during his brewing.

For more information about Scott Voak, visit http://www.VoakHomes.com.

Maximizing the Profit When Selling Your Home

By David Rudd and Emily Hervieux

Introduction

David Rudd and Emily Hervieux both have technical backgrounds. David has a business degree in high tech management and Emily has a degree in biology. After working in high tech and biotech companies David and Emily decided that they liked working with people, and by using their analytical skills they could provide a superior level of service helping buyers and sellers with their real estate transactions. They consistently rank among the top 1% among all real estate agents in San Diego County.

David and Emily are good students of the San Diego County real estate market and they keep up to date on buyer preferences. Over time they developed some unique techniques to maximize the sales price, and thus the profit, when their clients are selling their homes. In this chapter they provide an overview of these strategies that position their clients to make tens of thousands extra when selling their homes.

A Better Way to Sell Your Home

After years of reviewing and analyzing San Diego County home sales data we have observed that more than half of the time money is being left on the table. Sellers are missing out on making as much as 30 to 60 thousand dollars extra profit when they are selling their home, and they don't realize it. It makes us sick to see this as it's money that can be put into their next home, send a child to college, or to save for retirement. A different approach to selling is needed to realize this extra profit.

When a homeowner is ready to sell their property, the typical approach is to talk to one or more real estate agents to see what they think the home is worth. The agent(s) will tour the property, will bring along some recent sales data, and come up with an estimated amount that they think the home is worth. This has been a pretty common practice for decades in our industry. Rather than telling you what your home is worth we take a different approach—showing you exactly what you can do to make your home worth more, so that you're assured the sale will be as profitable as possible. We consider the following concepts important to maximize the value and the profit: intelligent fix-up, staging, marketing, and negotiation.

To give some perspective of how effective this process is, when you look at all our past sales within the last twelve months, over 70% of the time we get more than one offer within the first two weeks of showings.

Intelligent Fix-up

After years of observing home sales in the area we've seen that there's generally a big opportunity to increase the value of your property and home preparation is one of the most significant factors. We have developed a concept to make appropriate changes that we call "intelligent fix-up." With intelligent fix-up we identify specific changes to a home that will generate at least three dollars in a home sale for every dollar invested. It's usually just a few items that can be handled in a short period of time before the home goes on the market. A 3-to-1 return is pretty good and we are helping sellers get tens of thousands of dollars of additional profit from their home sale using this technique.

Every home is different and it takes a trained eye and knowledge of what buyers are looking for to identify small improvements that will return three-to-one. To better understand the concept of intelligent fix-up we have elaborated below some fairly typical examples. It's important to point out that styles change frequently, so while some of the preferred colors mentioned here are currently in style as we are writing this, it's not a specific guide for the longer-term.

The first step is to approach the home the way a buyer would, parking their car out front and walking up to the front door. First impressions are critical so pay attention to what buyers will experience walking up to the front door. Are the walk and driveway clean? Power washing will make them look like new again. Look around the structure itself. Stucco and the eaves may also benefit from power washing. If you have shrubs or hedges near the walk, make sure they're trimmed back so buyers don't have to dodge past them to get to the front door. The front door itself is very important. We live in such a sunny climate that doors that are painted or stained tend to fade over time. So, we'll often recommend putting on a fresh coat of paint or stain to give it a nice pop of color. Also check the door hardware to make sure it opens easily. Homeowners tend to come and go through the garage, and the front door may not be operated very often. What we don't want to happen is for an agent to be showing your home and it's difficult to unlock. That subconsciously will set a negative tone for that buyer's showing. You want them to come up to the front door, the door opens easily, and then they can begin their showing.

Once the entry door opens there's usually an area with tile that transitions to carpeting or hardwood flooring. The tile is typically in good shape because there's generally not much traffic through the front door, but oftentimes the tile is dated. It's been there for maybe twenty or thirty years and it might have been installed when darker colors were the preferred style. It's usually a small area and it often makes sense to remove and put in a lighter tile that's going to modernize the look of the entry area. There's a series of affordable Onyx Sand porcelain tiles that buyers are really appreciating. We recommend using 12" x 24" tiles set in a brick pattern because it creates an open feeling, making the space seem larger.

Sometimes we will see a bathroom or a laundry area that has vinyl flooring. Even if you have lots of upgrades in your home, and you have one room with vinyl flooring, buyers are going to leave the property thinking that the home needs to be upgraded. These areas are usually small, so it can make sense to replace the vinyl with porcelain tile.

Another opportunity for intelligent fix-up is removal of popcorn ceilings and re-texturing the ceiling surfaces. There are two reasons for making this suggestion. Prior to 1978 asbestos was used in the manufacturing of the acoustic popcorn material. It's interesting that buyers see the popcorn ceilings, and even if the home was built in the '80s, they're going to think of health and safety issues as a result of the possibility of the asbestos content. The other reason is that a smooth ceiling brightens up the home. Multiple studies have shown that there is a direct correlation between how bright the home is and how much it sells for, so the brighter the better. When we get ready to start showings we recommend to remove the screens out of the windows that you're not using, just to bring in more natural light and make the home as bright as possible. Sometimes we will also recommend removal of window treatments, again to brighten the room.

A lot of homes have white baseboards and they get dinged and scuffed in high traffic areas like entryways, halls, and the kitchen. Instead of replacing them, just putting a fresh coat of a semi-gloss pure white paint will help to brighten things up. Usually the bedrooms don't get a lot of traffic so there's not as big of a need for repainting the baseboards in the bedrooms.

The kitchen is one of the most important rooms when it comes to attracting buyers and a good offer for your home. Kitchen remodels are expensive so we rarely recommend significant updating, but there are often opportunities to increase value with some minor changes. Solid honey oak cabinets were pretty common in new construction twenty or thirty years ago. We see them in about 20 percent of the house being sold in the area, but the style is not something today's buyers desire. They are really solid and are very durable so replacing them is usually not the answer, especially considering the cost of new cabinets. They can be painted or stained with a nice crisp color. Oftentimes sellers think that it's a shame to paint the wood, but right now white or slightly off-white is what buyers want. There's a color that's popular with buyers and builders are using a lot right now called "impressive white." Regardless of the decision to paint and the color of the cabinets, another low cost intelligent fix up we suggest is adding pulls to the cabinets. At the same time replace the hinges to match the pulls. Attractive pulls really make the cabinets look better. If you have wood cabinets, brushed nickel or satin nickel work well. If you have white or ivory cabinets, we usually suggest oiled bronze. They provide a nice contrast with the white cabinets.

We generally don't recommend changing countertops or appliances unless there is damage to the countertops or the appliances are very old. As we discussed earlier, we rarely suggest complete kitchen makeovers due to the typical return on investment not meeting goals; however, there are a few homes every year we see where a full kitchen remodel would generate a good return. We'll discuss a specific case to give an example where a remodel would be justified. In this case the home had been a rental property for about ten years. Two years prior to meeting the owner, he had installed new panel windows, redone the bathrooms, and installed new flooring throughout. The kitchen was original from the '60s. We knew any prospective buyers coming through, would leave the showing thinking that the kitchen needs to be redone and would likely discount their offer by 30 to 50 thousand dollars because of the condition of the kitchen. We were able to recommend cabinets, countertops, and new appliances that ended up costing around $10,000 installed. So, in this situation the seller was able to achieve at least a 300 percent return on the investment.

We would not generally consider refinishing any cabinets outside the kitchen unless they are in line of sight from the kitchen and contrast with the kitchen cabinets. We do suggest adding pulls to cabinets throughout the home, following the same scheme we mentioned for the kitchen. This dresses up the built-in cabinets and is very inexpensive. Contractor packs sold at the big box home improvement stores are pretty economical. Builders today are not using brass doorknobs or pulls so while looking through the home, consider paring down the use of brass hardware to modernize the appearance of the home. We would suggest using satin nickel or oiled bronze for doorknobs.

Another process that is consistent with a three-to-one return is bath fixture refinishing. Back in the '80s and '90s many new homes had colored bathtubs and sinks. Today's standard and what buyers prefer is brilliant white. There are companies that specialize in refinishing tubs, sinks, and shower pans, and they can change them to a brilliant white in one day. Older shower pans that are fiberglass often cannot be cleaned to return them to white again no matter how much you clean them, and this is another solution for off-color showers. Refinishing also works for repairing chipped tubs and fixing cast iron tubs with rust spots. This is another cost-effective way to modernize the home without a big demolition project and the end result is all of the refinished fixtures will look new.

Cultured marble vanity countertops are nice, but over time they tend to yellow. So, instead of replacing, they can be refinished as well. The companies that refinish cultured marble have a process that makes the countertops look like granite. Refinishing just takes a few hours and for a cost that is usually in the range of $200 to $300 you can really revamp the look of a bathroom.

Again, remember what we have described above is representative of typical intelligent fix ups we might recommend. Every home is different and we suggest that before you start making changes you talk with an expert in current buyer preferences and who has the experience to know where you can generate at least a three-to-one payback in any changes you make to your property.

Staging

Once the intelligent fix ups are completed, the next step is to stage the home. Think about staging as builders showcase their model homes. They decorate with very attractive color schemes and nice furnishings, making for a pleasant showing experience. Compare that to the same model home in the development that is vacant and echoes while you are walking through it. The purpose of staging is to improve the presentation for in-person showings and also to elevate the caliber of the photos used in all of the marketing pieces that will be used to increase the amount of interest and to generate showings.

Staging is really important, especially for a vacant home. We never want to sell a home that's empty for a couple of reasons. Rooms that don't have furniture in them actually look smaller than rooms that have appropriately sized furniture, especially when you're looking at a master bedroom. You could walk past the master and think the room is too small and your furniture is not going to fit. But if you have a queen-size bed and nightstands and dresser and there is still plenty of room to walk around it, people realize that their things will, in fact, fit. Another reason that we always like to stage vacant homes is that if you walk into an empty room, naturally your eyes will scan the room. And your eye will get drawn to any little imperfection. So if there's a little stain on the carpet, or if there's a ding in the drywall, that's where your eye is going to go, and that's what you're going to remember from your showing. As opposed to stepping into a beautiful room, and you see nice furnishings, area rugs, plants, and decorative items. You walk in and the room feels good. And that's what you remember and that's what you take away from your showing.

HomeGain, a national real estate services company, recently completed a study on sales prices for staged vs. unstaged homes. They found that the staged homes on average sold for 12% more than unstaged homes. This was a national study and the average sales price was $400,000. So, if your home were worth a million dollars, it wouldn't necessarily mean that you can expect an extra 12% return, but the bottom line is that staged homes consistently sell for more money. The same study by HomeGain found that staged homes sold for more money and also found that staged homes spent less time on the market - 83% less time compared to unstaged properties. We believe in staging, because it gives our clients more money, and it's less hassle for them, as they don't have to have their home on the market for an extended period of time.

Knowing that staged homes sell for more money and in a shorter period of time, one would think that all real estate agents would stage properties. The truth is that it's not happening. The main reason is because of the cost associated with it. If you hire a staging company to stage a 2500 square foot home, on average, it would cost about $3000 to $4000 for the first 90 days and then monthly payment after that, if the furniture needs to stay there longer. In our case, we truly believe that our duty to our clients is to sell their property for as much money as possible and we know staging really helps make that happen. To resolve this, over the last several years we've acquired our own staging inventory. So we have a warehouse right here in the area and we offer to our clients to stage their property for free. We approach staging two different ways. If your home is vacant, then we're going to bring furnishings for all the main living areas and the master bedroom. If your home is occupied then we will compliment whatever you have. So, we might determine that some furnishing are a little too large for the area and we might swap a few pieces just to make your home show to it's full potential.

Decluttering is also an important part of staging the home. Homeowners generally have accumulated a lot of things and bookshelves and mantles are full. As a general rule we suggest removing about half of what you have in these places, opening up some space. When arranging furniture, it's important to make sure there is plenty of space for potential buyers to easily maneuver as they are walking through the house. We have a concept that we call the "suitcase test," which can be used as you are laying out the furniture, preparing for showings. Think of carrying a suitcase on each side and make sure there is enough space to walk throughout the home and not running into any of the furniture with the suitcases. This may seem like a rather wide pathway, but it will ensure that buyers have enough space to meander between pieces of furniture.

Marketing by Presenting and Exposing the Property to the Most Potential Qualified Buyers

Once the staging is complete, it a matter of capturing all of the home's beauty to expose it to as many qualified buyers as possible. Real estate marketing has mostly gone online over the past ten years. Currently 92% of the buyers are online and they're using sites like Zillow or Realtor.com to identify candidate properties. They're in front of a computer, looking at photos to determine which home they're going to go and look at in person. Even the dynamic between a buyer and agent has changed dramatically. It used to be the agent would send or show their clients a list of different available properties. But now, most buyers have one or more apps and they're pinged as soon as a new listing comes up that matches their parameters. They are more likely to be flipping through the photos to decide which homes they like, and then they contact their agent to indicate which ones they want to see in person. Presentation makes a tremendous difference in attracting buyers' interest in an in-person showing.

High quality photos are super important and we hire a professional photographer to take photos that are very crisp and bright. Proper lighting conditions are critical for the best presentation. Our photographer takes a rapid sequence of three photos for every image we will be using and then in the office an associate combines the three photos to extract the brightness and contrast to make the colors vibrant. These are known as High Dynamic Range or HDR photos. Aerial videos are very effective, especially when we are trying to describe the view. It's one thing to write about canyon or ocean views, but when we're able to display the view in a video it's a lot more engaging and powerful.

With high quality photography and videos completed we can now list the home in the Multiple Listing Service (MLS). MLS listings are syndicated to hundreds of websites including Zillow, Realtor.com, and Trulia, but there are big differences in how well the property is displayed on these websites, depending on the agent's membership subscription level. The most common arrangement is that four photos can be displayed for each property, but that doesn't give buyers much of a feel for the home. We have premium showcase listing memberships to these sites, so we can display up to 35 photos as well as videos. We've been keeping track of our numbers over the past several years, and we are getting an offer on average for every seven to eight showings that we get. By capturing the attention of qualified buyers online we've been creating quality showings that result in a fairly high ratio of offers to showings.

Another way to increase exposure is to make a property website for the home. We use a URL that matches the address and we add a small sign at the top of the for sale sign with the web address that's easy to see. The property website has all of the data and specs on the house and interested buyers can click a button to schedule a showing. We find that this is a wonderful tool for neighbors to help sell a home. It's not uncommon for you to have a neighbor who has a colleague at work, or a family member, looking to move into the neighborhood. Instead of just grabbing a flier with a few pictures, they can send them to the property site where they can get all of the information and schedule the showing with us directly.

It's important to understand where buyers are coming from and each year more and more buyers from outside of the United States are buying in San Diego County. It's now over 10% of buyers. The five main countries they're coming from are Canada, Mexico, UK, India, and China. So at Keller Williams we have a program called Buyers Without Borders, and we have exclusive right to syndicate our listings to 84 MLS systems outside of the U.S. With this access, our listings are translated into the native language, and end up reaching 500,000 agents outside of the United States. Whereas in San Diego County we have 20 to 25 thousand agents, being able to advertise our clients' property to an additional 500,000 agents around the world is a pretty broad reach. Every month we sell two to three homes to international buyers. For the most part international buyers are paying cash. We observe that oftentimes they are low maintenance compared to a local buyer, so it tends to be a lot smoother through the escrow process. Most people think of cash buyers as investors that typically are making low ball offers, but we don't find that to be the case with international buyers.

Negotiation

When considering what makes for a skilled negotiation it's really important to understand buyer psychology. When a buyer decides to make an offer, they're at their peak of excitement and enthusiasm. But over time that excitement diminishes. We want to negotiate with the buyer that is mentally moving into the home. In that frame of mind, they're going to compromise more on price and terms than at any other point. So, the challenge we found with traditional negotiation is it takes way too long. By default when a buyer writes an offer, they give the seller three days to respond. As the seller, you will rarely accept an offer outright. You'll probably send a counteroffer changing the price or changing some of the terms. Then there's another three days to respond. And then maybe the buyer doesn't accept it, so a couple of times back and forth and you can eat up a week or two. You have a motivated buyer, but because of the time lag, the buyer is maybe looking at more houses now before making the final decision.

The traditional way of negotiating a home sale just takes too much time and oftentimes the buyer gets disengaged. Our goal is to negotiate the highest and best offer out of every buyer and when you take into account the buyer psychology component, you cannot wait to get that best offer a week later - you need to obtain it within the first 24 to 48 hours. We use what we call the "up front negotiation technique." It's a method to create a sense of urgency in the buyer.

When a buyer wants to see a listing, their agent contacts us and generally asks a simple question, "Is the property still available?" Instead of just answering yes or no, we want to create some urgency and demand for the property. We will describe the activity on the property, the time the property has been on the market (it's usually a short period), how many showings we've had, and if there has been significant interest in the feedback we have received, we might say something like, "At the rate of activity that we're getting, we're probably going to be in escrow within the next few days. If you have a very serious buyer, yes, absolutely, it is available right now if you come in today or tomorrow." Of course we always tell the truth on the actual activity level, but many times the selling agent doesn't say anything about the activity, they just report whether or not the property is still available. Once the showing takes place, if the buyers like the home, usually the agent will contact us and indicate that they liked the home and are thinking of putting in an offer. This is an opportunity to increase the urgency, especially if you've had additional activity. It's another time to describe the activity level and if you've had an offer or a buyer wanting a second showing you can indicate this, with a recommendation that if the buyer is as excited as is being conveyed, we would recommend to come in at full price and not wait to make an offer.

So, by having this conversation, we're able to get their initial offer at the level at what would've been counter offer number one, or even possibly counter offer number two. In most cases, we are able to get a deal done with only one counter offer and we're able to truly get the highest offer from that buyer.

What Sellers Are Saying

"Our "plan" was just to go and get educated and quickly leave without making any commitments to them before we began

interviewing several real estate agents first. However, after listening to their excellent and informative "no pressure" presentation, we were pleasantly shocked knowing we no longer needed to go through the process of checking out anyone else and we immediately hired them! Not once did we ever look back because of their dedication and expertise shown through the entire time selling our home.

From the first day we worked with Kindred-Hervieux to the last, they were incredible and consistently exceeded our expectations with their knowledge, work ethic, enthusiasm and dedication to us, their clients. We had a close to full price offer the very first day! We are extremely grateful for their suggestions and guidance through every step. They are a remarkable team!"

- K. Murdoch

"We highly recommend Kindred-Hervieux. They were wonderfully easy to work with, very professional as well as warm and caring. The house sold much more quickly than we expected, and for a much higher price! When the sale hit a few bumps along the way to the closing, they were always available to research and reassure – it made all the difference! We would use them again if we were to return to the San Diego area."

- J. & A. Clare

"I am writing in reference to the outstanding job Kindred-Hervieux did for us. With their help, we sold our home & bought another. We have kids in school and were nervous about selling our house and buying because we didn't want to move twice. Paul & Emily coordinated everything to make the sale and purchase smooth and easy. It was an absolute pleasure working with them on both

transactions. They were extremely responsive with all phone calls & emails. It is difficult to find competent professionals and both Paul & Emily far exceeded my expectations. I highly recommend working with them and look forward to working with Kindred-Hervieux in the future."

- A. Swartz

"We cannot thank Kindred-Hervieux enough for all that they've done for us. We are in a better place in our life because of their help. They sold our home in less than a week, received multiple offers and sold it for more than we ever expected. Each step of the way, their care & generosity made such a complicated & stressful process, all that much easier. Their patience & guidance for us has been invaluable. Most importantly, from day one always felt like they treated us with the highest priority."

- A. Euben

"We would like to take this opportunity to extend our most sincere appreciation and gratitude for the support, assistance and friendship provided in the course of the sale of our home. Your patience and knowledge were invaluable in bringing the sale to a successful conclusion. From our initial meeting we were impressed by your 'realty savvy' and also with your warmth & genuine interested in making the process as easy as possible. We cannot say enough about your responsiveness to our needs, and your availability whenever we had questions or concerns. You never failed to return our calls or emails promptly. We look forward to working with you again in the future!"

- S. Abitz

"When a friend found out that we were ready to sell our house, he highly recommended Kindred-Hervieux at Keller Williams Realty. Their team began helping us even before we signed any paperwork. Selling a house is a very stressful time and they helped calm us by being very reassuring and explaining everything each step of the way. They ended up selling our house for $25,000 more than the last sale in the community, we couldn't be happier! I would highly recommend Kindred-Hervieux due to our great experience."

- J. Mondry

About David Rudd

David has worked in both the real estate acquisition and sales and the construction and remodeling fields. This extensive experience allows him to offer a complete living space management service, providing expertise in seeking out ideal properties in addition to construction and renovation know-how, and a deep understanding of the sales process.

David is one that likes to know everything about an industry, so he has also been licensed as a home appraiser, general contractor and worked in the lending business as well. The depth of this additional knowledge benefits his clients and his team by thoroughly understanding all aspects of the real estate transaction. Originally drawn to San Diego for its warm climate compared to Lincoln, Nebraska, David quickly found the people to be equally warm.

After working years in high tech and running operations for regional tech companies, David returned to his passion of real estate.

Now he brings his high tech precision and the focus, discipline, and dedication he developed and perfected to his work in residential acquisitions and sales and living space adaptations. David's ability to provide a complete service package gives his clients maximum flexibility and efficiency in choosing and crafting the perfect home for their needs.

For more information about David Rudd, visit http://www.KindredRE.com.

About Emily Hervieux

Emily's passion for real estate is undeniable. As a Realtor and investor, she brings her creative and unique perspective to each and every client. Whether it's buying or selling, she smoothly and harmoniously sees each transaction through to completion. Her knowledge, diligence and finely tuned skills set her apart from other real estate professionals.

Emily and her husband have invested in real estate for years. Their portfolio includes single-family homes, duplexes, building lots, and they recently acquired a 14,000 sq. ft. commercial building in Phoenix.

Outside of working with clients, Emily's family is the center of her world. Both she and her husband raced triathlon and continue to enjoy training for leisure. They have been married for almost 10 years and have two young children.

Emily brings her mid-western work ethic to Southern California and begins each day at 5 a.m. Her accumulation of passion, steadfast determination, and innovative and aggressive marketing strategies allows her to find exceptional deals for her clients and sell homes quickly.

Buying and Selling Homes in La Mesa and East San Diego County

By Maggie Clemens

Introduction

Maggie Clemens grew up in Downers Grove, Illinois and she joined the U.S. Navy directly out of high school, excited to see the world while working towards a college degree. The Navy sent her to San Diego. As much as she was hoping for an overseas station she fell in love with San Diego as she saw the twinkling lights of the harbor. As she toured the city that day she knew she was going to be staying.

During five years in the Navy at what was then Naval Air Station (NAS) Miramar, Maggie earned a B.S. in Computer Science. After leaving the Navy she worked in the computer science industry for 3 years, but quickly tired of sitting in front of a computer all day. A friend suggested she try car sales as a temporary filler job. The "temporary" job lasted almost 25 years, where her easy manner and excellent customer service earned her many repeat clients and referrals.

Maggie started buying and investing in real estate at the age of 25 and began to closely follow the San Diego market. Her strong negotiation background coupled with her local real estate knowledge made a second career in real estate an ideal match. Helping others to buy, sell, and invest in real estate is her passion. She has clients all over San Diego County, but her primary focus is in La Mesa and East County.

In this chapter, Maggie provides insights for both homebuyers as well as sellers in the area surrounding La Mesa and also East San Diego County.

Selling Your La Mesa or East County Home

Selling a home is one of the largest transactions most people will make in their lifetime. Yet data provided by the National Association of Realtors (N.A.R.) indicates that over 70% of all people planning on selling their property only talk to one agent or broker prior to listing their home for sale. It is best to realize that your home is an asset and the only way to know that you have hired the right agent is to talk to a couple. A second opinion will give you better answers and a better understanding of the process and marketing.

Once you have the right agent, it's a good idea to meet with that agent as soon as the decision has been made to sell. An agent will be able to walk thru the home and provide insight on some of the small things that can make a property more attractive to buyers and thus sell for the highest amount in the shortest time. I call this the Home Value Audit. Many times, a small investment of time, at minimal cost invested in the home, can be an attractive return on the investment. The earlier the agent is involved the more time to complete any updates with less stress.

A home has about 8 seconds to make an impression when a prospective buyer drives up to the front of that property, so curb appeal is critical. It may be just adding a few plants with color and re-painting the front door to make a great first impression. Preparing the inside of your home for potential buyers is another critical step. As a buyer tours your home it is only natural for them to try to visualize it as their home. The more neutral and de-cluttered your home is, the easier it is for the buyer to see their furniture and picture their life in the home. Unusual colors can limit buyers' interest, so it is best to consider painting walls that have very dark or unusual colors to something more neutral.

Price is one of the most important aspects when it comes to selling a home. There's so much information available online now and you can see what your neighbors' homes have sold for as well as listing prices on most homes currently on the market. It may seem like an easy process, but establishing the right price range is more of an art. A professional agent will prepare a Comparative Market Analysis (CMA). The CMA will include pricing for the most similar homes that have recently sold as well as for similar homes currently on the market, adjusting the prices to reflect conditions of the sellers' home. It will also include an analysis of the market situation, such as the inventory of homes on the market and the average days on market. The other point to consider is what an appraiser will look at and how an appraiser will evaluate the home, as an appraisal will be required on any transactions where the buyer will be financing the purchase.

A lot of sellers will look at online sites that provide property price estimates. These sites provide a general guide, not necessarily very accurate, and the algorithm doesn't reflect actual conditions of the property. Like most online information these days insight is still required to interpret the data properly. It is the agent's job to provide the hard facts on what the true value of the house is worth at the time it's ready to list. Although some people think that the agent sets the price, it is really the homeowners that decide what they want it listed for, after hearing all the analysis provided by the agent.

Proper pricing as well as the market condition will affect how long it will take for a listed property to sell. Markets change based on supply and demand, overall economic conditions, and mortgage rates. For the past few years as this is being written, the overall market in San Diego County has had a relatively tight inventory, so it has been a seller's market. Even in a seller's market, it's important to price at the market price or the seller may not get many interested buyers or offers. In today's market the home that is priced right will attract more viewings and generally one or more offers within a short period of time. Over time, market conditions may change to the point where supply and demand are more in balance and there are more homes for buyers to choose from; when that happens, pricing the home right will be even more important. How fast a home will sell also depends on the marketing methods deployed.

Homeowners often ask me if their home needs to be in perfect condition before they list it for sale. Most buyers are not expecting a property to be in perfect condition; however, it's still important to make as good of a first impression as possible. In addition to neutral colors, one of the most important things is to de-clutter and de-personalize the home so buyers can imagine living in the home themselves. We also want to make sure the windows and carpets are clean and the house is tidy in all the rooms. There are a lot of little touch-ups, like making sure all the lights and fans work, or touching up paint that can be done for little cost. I talked earlier about curb appeal, and the first impression from the street or driveway as potential buyers are walking in is very important. Big impressions are made in just the first few seconds.

If the house is empty, it should be staged with some furnishings so buyers can get a better idea of how the home would look. In my experience a home that is staged will sell quicker than a vacant home. Even if the seller is living in the home, it's a good idea to stage some of the rooms so buyers can imagine other uses of certain rooms. An example of this would be a spare bedroom could be staged as an office, craft room, or baby's' room. A general theme is to make the home as neutral as possible so that buyers walking through can see the different possibilities in their minds.

Sometimes it's a good idea for the seller to have a home inspection and maybe a termite inspection prior to putting the property on the market, especially if there is some concern about condition. Having inspections completed in advance can be beneficial by showing them to buyers indicating that potential issues have been addressed already. This is another way to make the home more attractive, especially if it's an older home.

Knowing how buyers are typically finding their homes helps to devise a good marketing strategy. This changes over time, and every year I examine the data provided by the National Association of Realtors that profiles the homebuyers and sellers. Use of the Internet is increasing every year by buyers in the area. Exposure in online listing sites as well as on Social Media sites are becoming critical to getting your home seen by buyers. We still use some older techniques like flyers and talking with other agents to get more exposure.

With so many buyers looking online at homes for sale, professional photography is critical to make the home attractive to buyers. Everything we do in marketing from the online exposure to Facebook and even flyers are based on great photos to showcase the home.

Once we have great photos, the next step is to pre-market the home before the listing goes lives to generate quick interest. An open house for agents is one of the best ways to do this, especially in a strong market, as a lot of agents are searching for the ideal home for their clients. We will also hold an open house for buyers and heavily promote the open house right before or as the listing is going active. Pre-marketing activity many times can generate one or more offers in a matter of days.

Although the San Diego area doesn't really have any winter weather, homes sales activity slows down significantly in November and December. Most homeowners don't want to have to keep the house clean during the holidays or have people viewing their home when they have gifts lying around. There are still buyers looking for a home during this time and with inventory traditionally low, there's less competition for sellers. Buyers are typically going to look at 12 to 15 houses before they make a decision. During the holiday period with fewer homes on the market, they may only be able to see about 6 to 8 that fit their criteria, thus the competition for homes listed at this time is much lower. This is another point to consider if it's nearing the end of the year and you have a desire to sell during that time.

What Sellers Are Saying

"Maggie helped my partner and I sell our home in Talmadge as quickly as possible so that we could get to our new home in the Desert where we are enjoying Retired Life and Complete Freedom!

She set up an open house for investors only on a Friday and just 3 days later, on Monday afternoon we had received 3 offers! We accepted an offer and closed escrow in only 3 weeks

She was excellent at keeping us informed every step of the way and was instrumental in finding a company to help us clean out our Talmadge home as soon as possible.

I would recommend Maggie's real estate services to anyone looking to sell their home or purchase the home of their dreams!"

- Steve W.

"Working with Maggie in the sale of my home was a great experience! She is caring, organized, detailed, upfront, honest, and follows through with what she says. I will continue to work with her on all my future home transactions, and I would not hesitate to recommend her to anyone!"

- Judy

"I have been in contact with Maggie for over a year via email. When it was time for me to sell my property I called her and we met in person. She walked through the entire process of selling my property and what to expect considering I had a renter in my house. She forged a good relationship with my renter to ensure I got the best possible buyers for my property. Within days of listing my property we had several offers. I was very impressed with the knowledge, expertise and professionalism Maggie had throughout the process. I will definitely use Maggie the next time I purchase a property. Thanks Maggie! You are awesome!"

- Sonya

Buying Your La Mesa or East County Home

The Internet has forever changed the way that real estate is presented and most buyers start searching online well before they are ready to make a decision, unless they have an immediate need such as relocating for a job. When you're getting serious about finding a home, it's time to interview a couple of agents and make a decision on the agent you will be relying on to guide you through the home buying process. Some people think that they can just find a house online and work with the listing agent to complete a transaction. While that is possible, remember that the listing agent has a fiduciary responsibility to the seller, not the buyer, so no one would be looking out for you, the buyer, in such case. The seller is paying the commission on both sides of the transaction, so there is no savings to the buyer if the buyer doesn't have their own agent as the full commission would go to the listing agent.

A buyer's agent will be able to provide a good foundation on the current market situation and make sure you're not overpaying. Knowledge about the current market dynamics gives a better understanding of the competitiveness of the local real estate market, which is important in structuring offers. You may have heard of buyer's markets and seller's markets and supply vs. demand. When available housing inventory is low and there are lots of buyers looking for a home, it's a seller's market and buyers will need to make a very good offer to get preference over other buyers. In fact, there will likely be multiple offers for a property. In the opposite situation, when inventory is high relative to the number of buyers shopping for a home, sellers are competing for buyers and it's a buyer's market. In this case sellers have to be more flexible and may need to compromise a lot more. Local markets generally normalize over time, but as we are writing this, the San Diego area has been in a very competitive seller's market for a few years now.

A buyer's agent will also guide a buyer through all of the paperwork and inspections, help structure a competitive offer, and be advocating for the buyer in the negotiations.

It's very important in a tight market to have the strongest offer on a house you want to buy. A critical component of that is having mortgage pre-approval before actively looking at houses. For the most part, sellers are not going to consider offers that are contingent on the buyer having to obtain a mortgage. With pre-approval, a borrower takes that issue off of the table. The borrower submits all of the documentation necessary for a loan and the lender will go through the underwriting process, verifying all the information, and issue financing approval up to a certain amount. This means that the only variable left is the appraisal of the property to make sure the value is in line with the lending guidelines. It's like walking around with a blank check and you can essentially buy any house up to the amount approved.

You may hear about loan pre-qualification, but that's not as strong as pre-approval. With pre-qualification, the borrower only provides information to the lender, not the documentation that is required for approval, and the lender will issue a pre-qualification letter based on the information that is supplied. Since a lender does not review and verify any documentation, pre-qualification is not nearly as strong as pre-approval.

Like most agents that work with buyers, I have a selection of lenders I can recommend to homebuyers. That's another reason to start working with an agent when you're about ready to actively look for a home.

Negotiations are a necessary part of purchasing a home and an experienced agent can help you structure a strong offer and guide you through the transaction process. Some buyers think that a low-ball offer is the way to get the negotiations going. Although that can be effective when there is excessive inventory and the property has stalled on the market for a long time, most of the time properties are priced in an appropriate range and in tight markets like we have been experiencing, a low-ball offer won't even get considered. In our area sales are rarely less than 90% of the list price. So, offering much less than 90% of the list price probably won't get a response. We have been in a seller's market for some time and well priced, attractive properties are receiving multiple offers. In this situation only the strongest offers will be considered.

In California the buyer has 17 days to complete all of the due diligence and remove contingencies on the accepted offer. In that 17 days the buyer needs to review all of the seller disclosures, determine if they are comfortable with what the seller is disclosing, have inspections completed, and review all Home Owner Association (HOA) documents, if applicable. During that 17-day period the buyer can back out of the agreement and have the earnest money returned.

Seventeen days sounds like a lot of time, but I always advise my clients to get the home inspection completed immediately. One reason is that some findings in the inspection may indicate that a more specialized inspection is needed, for instance if a suspected problem is found with the plumbing or an HVAC system. In such a case, you may want to have a specialist do a more thorough inspection of these systems. Additional inspections will take more time so it's best to start right away.

No home is going to be perfect but you want to buy your home with your eyes wide open and know if there are potential issues. They may not be major issues that you're going to require the seller to repair, but you should have a good idea about the condition of the property and all the systems. All houses need updating and maintenance and inspections are the best way to determine the current condition and are a good indicator of how well the seller has maintained the property.

In the East County beyond La Mesa we have more of a rural environment. A lot of people moving into the rural areas are moving from more urban areas in San Diego County or from outside the area. A big difference in most of the rural communities is the lack of the same public utilities one is used to in the cities. Many properties have private septic systems instead of city sewer and many also have a well for water. Natural gas is generally not going to be available and propane is used instead. This will require a conversion of a dryer that is made for natural gas fuel. In addition to the standard home inspections, a full septic system inspection and also a well water test is recommended during your due diligence period. Knowing the important things to watch for when considering rural community properties is another reason to work with an agent, especially one that is familiar with the different conditions likely to be encountered in many of the East County areas.

One of the things to look for on the seller's disclosure statement is natural hazard disclosure. We have some areas in the county, particularly in the eastern parts, that are designated as fire hazard zones. Due to the higher fire risks in these zones, some insurance companies will not insure in these zones. Also you can expect that the homeowners insurance will require a higher premium so this is something to take into consideration at the time of a decision to purchase properties in designated fire hazard zones.

In California after an agreement is reached on a real estate sale, escrow is opened. The escrow company is an independent third party that facilitates all of the aspects of the transaction and holds money to be dispersed at closing. They make sure that all aspects of the contract are completed before closing and disbursing funds. An important part of the transaction is making sure that clear title can be transferred to the buyer and a title company is involved to check for liens on the property and make sure that any that are found are cleared before the closing. Many times the seller is not aware of liens and only after the escrow is opened and the title company does a title check are liens discovered. It's fairly easy in California for someone to go to a recorder's office and record a lien, particularly in the case of a Mechanic's Lien.

What Buyers Are Saying

"Maggie did a thorough and professional job in helping us find our beautiful new home! I would not hesitate to work with her again in the future. She was on top of any problems that arose and did a great job in smoothing them out."

- Byron & Lynne

"Maggie went above and beyond helping us find the perfect place. She was patient and worked incredibly hard to find exactly what we were looking for."

- Tom

"There aren't enough words to describe what a wonderful Realtor Maggie is. In addition to being a 100% top-notch professional, she is a great listener, and true pleasure to be with.

My husband and I first started working with her from out-of-state. We were totally unfamiliar with San Diego and Maggie was instrumental in helping us get a feel for the neighborhoods and various housing options. We felt so comfortable with her, knowing we were in such professional and experienced hands, that we purchased our first San Diego property without stepping foot in it or meeting Maggie in person! Buying from across the country isn't easy, but Maggie did so much to help us... above and beyond what we'd ever experienced with a Realtor.

Within a year of moving to San Diego, we decided to purchase another home. Once again, it was Maggie to the rescue. (Except this time, she had to deal with my husband and me in person. This can sometimes be difficult, but I am convinced that Maggie doubles as a marriage counselor!) Just like before, Maggie found us the perfect house in the perfect neighborhood.

I have recommended Maggie to many people. My husband and I would never use any other Realtor in San Diego. We just feel that we can't be in better hands than Maggie's."

- Ellie

How to Select an Agent to Work With

Whether you're buying or selling a home, you will be working closely with your agent for some time. Buying or selling a home is one of the more stressful events in life and you want to be comfortable knowing that the agent is going to be available to you to answer your questions every step of the way. Years of experience and a good track record helping buyers and sellers with successfully completed transactions are good indicators of expertise. A full time agent is an indicator that real estate is a true profession for the agent. Part-time agents may not be readily available to answer your questions or inquiries from other agents. Successful agents will also be able to provide a list of references that you can check.

Relevant experience in the specific area of a home being sold or an area of interest to the buyer is important to make sure the agent is familiar with conditions typical in the area. Sellers should ask how their home will be marketed to expose it to the most appropriate buyers so it can be sold at the highest price in the shortest time.

The La Mesa Area

La Mesa is known as the "Jewel of the Hill." It's only nine square miles and I think it's the best-kept secret in the county, although more and more people have been recognizing the attractiveness and deciding to move to the city. La Mesa is one of the most centrally located cities in all of San Diego County, with close access to freeways and you can get to about anywhere within the county in just 20 minutes or less. It's only ten miles from the coast. The temperature is moderate with some of the coastal influence. Just a few miles further inland, as you drop down into El Cajon Valley, it gets a lot hotter. Like all of the San Diego areas, there are a variety of active lifestyles and outdoor activities available. Golf is popular and we have several golf courses in the area.

The East County area has more of a rural character and some larger properties. You'll see a lot of equestrian estates and there are many opportunities for horse riding on trails throughout the area. There are also dirt bike trails as well as walking trails. San Diego County has many lakes for those who like fishing or boating. Property values are very high at the coast, and as one moves inland to La Mesa and beyond, prices decline and larger properties are generally available, compared to along the coast.

About Maggie Clemens

Maggie Clemens is the principal agent of the Clemens Real Estate Group, affiliated with Keller Williams in La Mesa, California. She helps buyers, sellers, and investors with their real estate transactions throughout San Diego County. Maggie combined a background in auto sales, where she had a great following due to her excellent customer service, with personal experience buying and investing in San Diego area real estate. She has earned the San Diego Magazine 5 Star Award in Customer Satisfaction 3 years running. She is also an active member of the San Diego Association of Realtors Housing Opportunities Committee.

Originally from Chicago, Maggie joined the U.S. Navy right out of high school and her initial assignment was at the NAS Miramar near San Diego. Although she expected to see the world while in the Navy, she fell in love with San Diego the day she arrived and has never left. While serving at Miramar she earned a B.S in Computer Science.

For more information about Maggie Clemens, visit www.MaggieClemens.com

Notes

Notes

Notes

www.ingramcontent.com/pod-product-compliance
Lightning Source LLC
Chambersburg PA
CBHW070246230526
45470CB00002B/490